Terence Rattigan

Born in 1911, a scholar at Harrow and at Trinity College, Oxford, Terence Rattigan had his first long-running hit in the West End at the age of twenty-five: *French Without Tears* (1936). His next play, *After the Dance* (1939), opened to euphoric reviews yet closed under the gathering clouds of war, but with *Flare Path* (1942) Rattigan embarked on an almost unbroken series of successes, with most plays running in the West End for at least a year and several making the transition to Broadway: *While the Sun Shines* (1943), *Love in Idleness* (1944), *The Winslow Boy* (1946), *The Drowning Version* (performed in double-bill with *Harlequinade*, 1948), *Who is Sylvia?* (1950), *The Deep Blue Sea* (1952), *The Sleeping Prince* (1953) and *Separate Tables* (1954). From the mid-fifties, with the advent of the 'Angry Young Men', he enjoyed less success on stage, though *Ross* (1960) and *In Praise of Love* (1973) were well received. As well as seeing many of his plays turned into successful films, Rattigan wrote a number of original plays for television from the fifties onwards. He was knighted in 1971 and died in 1977.

D0542442

Terence Rattigan

PLAYBILL

THE BROWNING VERSION
and
HARLEQUINADE

Introduced by
DAN REBELLATO

NICK HERN BOOKS
London
www.nickhernbooks.co.uk

A Nick Hern Book

This edition of *The Browning Version & Harlequinade* first published in Great Britain in 1994 by Nick Hern Books, The Glasshouse, 49a Goldhawk Road, London W12 8QP. *The Browning Version* and *Harlequinade* were both included in Volume Two of *The Collected Plays of Terence Rattigan* published in 1953 by Hamish Hamilton

Reprinted 2007, 2009, 2012 (twice)

Typeset by Country Setting, Kingsdown, Kent CT14 8ES
Printed in the UK by Mimeo Ltd, Huntingdon, Cambridgeshire PE29 6XX

A CIP catalogue record for this book is available from the British Library

ISBN 978 1 85459 710 6

Terence Rattigan (1911-1977)

Terence Rattigan stood on the steps of the Royal Court Theatre, on 8 May 1956, after the opening night of John Osborne's *Look Back in Anger*. Asked by a reporter what he thought of the play, he replied, with an uncharacteristic lack of discretion, that it should have been retitled 'Look how unlike Terence Rattigan I'm being.' [1] And he was right. The great shifts in British theatre, marked by Osborne's famous première, ushered in kinds of playwriting which were specifically unlike Rattigan's work. The pre-eminence of playwriting as a formal craft, the subtle tracing of the emotional lives of the middle classes – those techniques which Rattigan so perfected – fell dramatically out of favour, creating a veil of prejudice through which his work even now struggles to be seen.

Terence Mervyn Rattigan was born on 10 June 1911, a wet Saturday a few days before George V's coronation. His father, Frank, was in the diplomatic corps and Terry's parents were often posted abroad, leaving him to be raised by his paternal grandmother. Frank Rattigan was a geographically and emotionally distant man, who pursued a string of little-disguised affairs throughout his marriage. Rattigan would later draw on these memories when he created Mark St Neots, the bourgeois Casanova of *Who is Sylvia?* Rattigan was much closer to his mother, Vera Rattigan, and they remained close friends until her death in 1971.

Rattigan's parents were not great theatregoers, but Frank Rattigan's brother had married a Gaiety Girl, causing a minor family uproar, and an apocryphal story suggests that the 'indulgent aunt' reported as taking the young Rattigan to the theatre may have been this scandalous relation.[2] And when, in the summer of 1922, his family went to stay in the country cottage of the drama critic Hubert Griffiths, Rattigan avidly worked through his extensive library of playscripts. Terry went to Harrow in 1925, and there maintained both his somewhat illicit theatregoing habit and his insatiable reading, reputedly devouring every play in the school library. Apart from contemporary authors like Galsworthy, Shaw and Barrie, he also read the plays of Chekhov, a writer whose crucial influence he often acknowledged.[3]

His early attempts at writing, while giving little sign of his later sophistication, do indicate his ability to absorb and reproduce his own theatrical experiences. There was a ten-minute melodrama about the Borgias entitled *The Parchment*, on the cover of which the author recommends with admirable conviction that a suitable cast for this work might comprise 'Godfrey Tearle, Gladys Cooper, Marie Tempest, Matheson Lang, Isobel Elsom, Henry Ainley . . . [and] Noël Coward'.[4] At Harrow, when one of his teachers demanded a French playlet for a composition exercise, Rattigan, undaunted by his linguistic shortcomings, produced a full-throated tragedy of deception, passion and revenge which included the immortal curtain line: 'COMTESSE. (*Souffrant terriblement*.) Non! non! non! Ah non! Mon Dieu, non!'[5] His teacher's now famous response was 'French execrable: theatre sense first class'.[6] A year later, aged fifteen, he wrote *The Pure in Heart,* a rather more substantial play showing a family being pulled apart by a son's crime and the father's desire to maintain his reputation. Rattigan's ambitions were plainly indicated on the title pages, each of which announced the author to be 'the famous playwrite and author T. M. Rattigan.'[7]

Frank Rattigan was less than keen on having a 'playwrite' for a son and was greatly relieved when in 1930, paving the way for a life as a diplomat, Rattigan gained a scholarship to read History at Trinity, Oxford. But Rattigan's interests were entirely elsewhere. A burgeoning political conscience that had led him to oppose the compulsory Officer Training Corps parades at Harrow saw him voice pacifist and socialist arguments at college, even supporting the controversial Oxford Union motion 'This House will in no circumstances fight for its King and Country' in February 1933. The rise of Hitler (which he briefly saw close at hand when he spent some weeks in the Black Forest in July 1933) and the outbreak of the Spanish Civil War saw his radical leanings deepen and intensify. Rattigan never lost his political compassion. After the war he drifted towards the Liberal Party, but he always insisted that he had never voted Conservative, despite the later conception of him as a Tory playwright of the establishment.[8]

Away from the troubled atmosphere of his family, Rattigan began to gain in confidence as the contours of his ambitions and his identity moved more sharply into focus. He soon took advantage of the university's theatrical facilities and traditions. He joined The Oxford Union Dramatic Society (OUDS), where contemporaries included Giles Playfair, George Devine, Peter Glenville, Angus Wilson and Frith Banbury. Each year, OUDS ran a one-act play competition and in Autumn 1931 Rattigan submitted one. Unusually, it seems that this was a highly experi-mental effort, somewhat like Konstantin's piece in *The Seagull*. George Devine, the OUDS president, apparently told the young author, 'Some of it is absolutely smashing, but it goes too far'.[9] Rattigan was instead to make his first mark as a somewhat scornful reviewer for the student newspaper, *Cherwell*, and as a performer in the Smokers (OUDS's private revue club), where he adopted the persona and dress of 'Lady Diana Coutigan', a drag performance which allowed him to discuss leading members of the Society with a barbed camp wit.[10]

That the name of his Smokers persona echoed the contemporary phrase, 'queer as a coot', indicates Rattigan's new-found confidence in his homosexuality. In February 1932, Rattigan played a tiny part in the OUDS production of *Romeo and Juliet*, which was directed by John Gielgud and starred Peggy Ashcroft and Edith Evans (women undergraduates were not admitted to OUDS, and professional actresses were often recruited). Rattigan's failure to deliver his one line correctly raised an increasingly embarrassing laugh every night (an episode which he re-uses to great effect in *Harlequinade*). However, out of this production came a friendship with Gielgud and his partner, John Perry. Through them, Rattigan was introduced to theatrical and homosexual circles, where his youthful 'school captain' looks were much admired.

A growing confidence in his sexuality and in his writing led to his first major play. In 1931, he shared rooms with a contemporary of his, Philip Heimann, who was having an affair with Irina Basilevich, a mature student. Rattigan's own feelings for Heimann completed an eternal triangle that formed the basis of the play he co-wrote with Heimann, *First Episode*. This play was accepted for production in Surrey's "Q" theatre; it was respectfully received and subsequently transferred to the Comedy Theatre in London's West End, though carefully shorn of its homosexual subplot. Despite receiving only £50 from this production (and having put £200 into it), Rattigan immediately dropped out of college to become a full-time writer.

Frank Rattigan was displeased by this move, but made a deal with his son. He would give him an allowance of £200 a year for two years and let him live at home to write; if at the end of that period, he had had no discernible success, he would enter a more secure and respectable profession. With this looming deadline, Rattigan wrote quickly. *Black Forest*, an O'Neill-inspired play based on his experiences in Germany in 1933, is one of the three that have survived. Rather unwillingly, he collaborated with Hector Bolitho on an adaptation of the latter's novel, *Grey Farm*, which received a disastrous New York production in 1940. Another project was an adaptation of *A Tale of Two Cities*, written with Gielgud; this fell through at the last minute when Donald Albery, the play's potential producer, received a complaint from actor-manager John Martin-Harvey who was beginning a farewell tour of his own adaptation, *The Only Way*, which he had been performing for forty-five years. As minor compensation, Albery invited Rattigan to send him any other new scripts. Rattigan sent him a play provisionally titled *Gone Away*, based on his experiences in a French language Summer School in 1931. Albery took out a nine-month option on it, but no production appeared.

By mid-1936, Rattigan was despairing. His father had secured him
a job with Warner Brothers as an in-house screenwriter, which was
reasonably paid; but Rattigan wanted success in the theatre, and his
desk-bound life at Teddington Studios seemed unlikely to advance
this ambition. By chance, one of Albery's productions was
unexpectedly losing money, and the wisest course of action seemed
to be to pull the show and replace it with something cheap. Since
Gone Away required a relatively small cast and only one set, Albery
quickly arranged for a production. Harold French, the play's
director, had only one qualm: the title. Rattigan suggested *French
Without Tears*, which was immediately adopted.

After an appalling dress rehearsal, no one anticipated the rapturous
response of the first-night audience, led by Cicely Courtneidge's
infectious laugh. The following morning Kay Hammond, the show's
female lead, discovered Rattigan surrounded by the next day's
reviews. 'But I don't believe it', he said. 'Even *The Times* likes it.' [11]

French Without Tears played over 1000 performances in its three-
year run and Rattigan was soon earning £100 a week. He moved
out of his father's home, wriggled out of his Warner Brothers
contract, and dedicated himself to spending the money as soon as it
came in. Partly this was an attempt to defer the moment when he
had to follow up this enormous success. In the event, both of his
next plays were undermined by the outbreak of war.

After the Dance, an altogether more bleak indictment of the Bright
Young Things' failure to engage with the iniquities and miseries of
contemporary life, opened, in June 1939, to euphoric reviews; but
only a month later the European crisis was darkening the national
mood and audiences began to dwindle. The play was pulled in
August after only sixty performances. *Follow My Leader* was a
satirical farce closely based on the rise of Hitler, co-written with an
Oxford contemporary, Tony Goldschmidt (writing as Anthony
Maurice in case anyone thought he was German). It suffered an
alternative fate. Banned from production in 1938, owing to the
Foreign Office's belief that 'the production of this play at this time
would not be in the best interests of the country', [12] it finally
received its première in 1940, by which time Rattigan and
Goldschmidt's mild satire failed to capture the real fears that the
war was unleashing in the country.

Rattigan's insecurity about writing now deepened. An interest in
Freud, dating back to his Harrow days, encouraged him to visit a
psychiatrist that he had known while at Oxford, Dr Keith Newman.
Newman exerted a svengali-like influence on Rattigan and
persuaded the pacifist playwright to join the RAF as a means of
curing his writer's block. Oddly, this unorthodox treatment seemed
to have some effect; by 1941, Rattigan was writing again. On one
dramatic sea crossing, an engine failed, and with everyone forced

to jettison all excess baggage and possessions, Rattigan threw the hard covers and blank pages from the notebook containing his new play, stuffing the precious manuscript into his jacket.

Rattigan drew on his RAF experiences to write a new play, *Flare Path*. Bronson Albery and Bill Linnit who had both supported *French Without Tears* both turned the play down, believing that the last thing that the public wanted was a play about the war.[13] H. M. Tennent Ltd., led by the elegant Hugh 'Binkie' Beaumont, was the third management offered the script; and in 1942, *Flare Path* opened in London, eventually playing almost 700 performances. Meticulously interweaving the stories of three couples against the backdrop of wartime uncertainty, Rattigan found himself 'commended, if not exactly as a professional playwright, at least as a promising apprentice who had definitely begun to learn the rudiments of his job'.[14] Beaumont, already on the way to becoming the most powerful and successful West End producer of the era, was an influential ally for Rattigan. There is a curious side-story to this production; Dr Keith Newman decided to watch 250 performances of this play and write up the insights that his 'serial attendance' had afforded him. George Bernard Shaw remarked that such playgoing behaviour 'would have driven me mad; and I am not sure that [Newman] came out of it without a slight derange-ment'.[15] Shaw's caution was wise. In late 1945, Newman went insane and eventually died in a psychiatric hospital.

Meanwhile, Rattigan had achieved two more successes; the witty farce, *While the Sun Shines*, and the more serious, though politically clumsy, *Love in Idleness* (retitled *O Mistress Mine* in America). He had also co-written a number of successful films, including *The Day Will Dawn*, *Uncensored*, *The Way to the Stars* and an adaptation of *French Without Tears*. By the end of 1944, Rattigan had three plays running in the West End, a record only beaten by Somerset Maugham's four in 1908.

Love in Idleness was dedicated to Henry 'Chips' Channon, the Tory MP who had become Rattigan's lover. Channon's otherwise gossipy diaries record their meeting very discreetly: 'I dined with Juliet Duff in her little flat . . . also there, Sibyl Colefax and Master Terence Rattigan, and we sparkled over the Burgundy. I like Rattigan enormously, and feel a new friendship has begun. He has a flat in Albany'.[16] Tom Driberg's rather less discreet account fleshes out the story: Channon's 'seduction of the playwright was almost like the wooing of Danaë by Zeus – every day the playwright found, delivered to his door, a splendid present – a case of champagne, a huge pot of caviar, a Cartier cigarette-box in two kinds of gold . . . In the end, of course, he gave in, saying apologetically to his friends, "How can one *not?*" '.[17] It was a very different set in which Rattigan now moved, one that was wealthy and conservative, the very people he had criticised in *After the*

Dance. Rattigan did not share the complacency of many of
his friends, and his next play revealed a deepening complexity and
ambition.

For a long time, Rattigan had nurtured a desire to become respected
as a serious writer; the commercial success of *French Without
Tears* had, however, sustained the public image of Rattigan as a
wealthy young light comedy writer-about-town. [18] With *The
Winslow Boy*, which premièred in 1946, Rattigan began to turn this
image around. In doing so he entered a new phase as a playwright.
As one contemporary critic observed, this play 'put him at once
into the class of the serious and distinguished writer'.[19] The play,
based on the Archer-Shee case in which a family attempted to sue
the Admiralty for a false accusation of theft against their son,
featured some of Rattigan's most elegantly crafted and subtle
characterization yet. The famous second curtain, when the barrister
Robert Morton subjects Ronnie Winslow to a vicious interrogation
before announcing that 'The boy is plainly innocent. I accept the
brief', brought a joyous standing ovation on the first night. No less
impressive is the subtle handling of the concept of 'justice' and
'rights' through the play of ironies which pits Morton's liberal
complacency against Catherine Winslow's feminist convictions.

Two years later, Rattigan's *Playbill*, comprising the one-act plays
The Browning Version and *Harlequinade*, showed an ever
deepening talent. The latter is a witty satire of the kind of touring
theatre encouraged by the new Committee for the Encouragement
of Music and Arts (CEMA, the immediate forerunner of the Arts
Council). But the former's depiction of a failed, repressed Classics
teacher evinced an ability to choreograph emotional subtleties on
stage that outstripped anything Rattigan had yet demonstrated.

Adventure Story, which in 1949 followed hard on the heels of
Playbill, was less successful. An attempt to dramatize the
emotional dilemmas of Alexander the Great, Rattigan seemed
unable to escape the vernacular of his own circle, and the epic
scheme of the play sat oddly with Alexander's more prosaic
concerns.

Rattigan's response to both the critical bludgeoning of this play
and the distinctly luke-warm reception of *Playbill* on Broadway
was to write a somewhat extravagant article for the *New
Statesman*. 'Concerning the Play of Ideas' was a desire to defend
the place of 'character' against those who would insist on the pre-
eminence in drama of ideas.[20] The essay is not clear and is couched
in such teasing terms that it is at first difficult to see why it should
have secured such a fervent response. James Bridie, Benn Levy,
Peter Ustinov, Sean O'Casey, Ted Willis, Christopher Fry and
finally George Bernard Shaw all weighed in to support or condemn
the article. Finally Rattigan replied in slightly more moderate

terms to these criticisms insisting (and the first essay reasonably supports this) that he was not calling for the end of ideas in the theatre, but rather for their inflection through character and situation.[21] However, the damage was done (as, two years later, with his 'Aunt Edna', it would again be done). Rattigan was increasingly being seen as the arch-proponent of commercial vacuity.[22]

The play Rattigan had running at the time added weight to his opponents' charge. Originally planned as a dark comedy, *Who is Sylvia?* became a rather more frivolous thing both in the writing and the playing. Rattled by the failure of *Adventure Story*, and superstitiously aware that the new play was opening at the Criterion, where fourteen years before *French Without Tears* had been so successful, Rattigan and everyone involved in the production had steered it towards light farce and obliterated the residual seriousness of the original conceit.

Rattigan had ended his affair with Henry Channon and taken up with Kenneth Morgan, a young actor who had appeared in *Follow My Leader* and the film of *French Without Tears*. However, the relationship had not lasted and Morgan had for a while been seeing someone else. Rattigan's distress was compounded one day in February 1949, when he received a message that Morgan had killed himself. Although horrified, Rattigan soon began to conceive an idea for a play. Initially it was to have concerned a homosexual relationship, but Beaumont, his producer, persuaded him to change the relationship to a heterosexual one.[23] At a time when the Lord Chamberlain refused to allow any plays to be staged that featured homosexuality, such a proposition would have been a commercial impossibility. The result is one of the finest examples of Rattigan's craft. The story of Hester Collyer, trapped in a relationship with a man incapable of returning her love, and her transition from attempted suicide to groping, uncertain self-determination is handled with extraordinary economy, precision and power. The depths of despair and desire that Rattigan plumbs have made *The Deep Blue Sea* one of his most popular and moving pieces.

1953 saw Rattigan's romantic comedy *The Sleeping Prince*, planned as a modest, if belated, contribution to the Coronation festivities. However, the project was hypertrophied by the insistent presence of Laurence Olivier and Vivien Leigh in the cast and the critics were disturbed to see such whimsy from the author of *The Deep Blue Sea*.

Two weeks after its opening, the first two volumes of Rattigan's *Collected Plays* were published. The preface to the second volume introduced one of Rattigan's best-known, and most notorious creations: Aunt Edna. 'Let us invent,' he writes, 'a character, a nice respectable, middle-class, middle-aged, maiden lady, with time on her hands and the money to help her pass it'.[24] Rattigan

paints a picture of this eternal theatregoer, whose bewildered
disdain for modernism ('Picasso—"those dreadful reds, my dear,
and why three noses?" ')[25] make up part of the particular challenge
of dramatic writing. The intertwined commercial and cultural
pressures that the audience brings with it exert considerable force
on the playwright's work.

Rattigan's creation brought considerable scorn upon his head. But
Rattigan is neither patronizing nor genuflecting towards Aunt Edna.
The whole essay is aimed at demonstrating the crucial rôle of the
audience in the theatrical experience. Rattigan's own sense of
theatre was *learned* as a member of the audience, and he refuses to
distance himself from this woman: 'despite my already self-
acknowledged creative ambitions I did not in the least feel myself a
being apart. If my neighbours gasped with fear for the heroine
when she was confronted with a fate worse than death, I gasped
with them'.[26] But equally, he sees his job as a writer to engage in
a gentle tug-of-war with the audience's expectations: 'although
Aunt Edna must never be made mock of, or bored, or befuddled,
she must equally not be wooed, or pandered to or cosseted'.[27] The
complicated relation between satisfying and surprising this figure
may seem contradictory, but as Rattigan notes, 'Aunt Edna herself
is indeed a highly contradictory character'.[28]

But Rattigan's argument, as in the 'Play of Ideas' debate before it,
was taken to imply an insipid pandering to the unchallenging
expectations of his audience. Aunt Edna dogged his career from
that moment on and she became such a by-word for what theatre
should *not* be that in 1960, the Questors Theatre, Ealing, could title
a triple-bill of Absurdist plays, 'Not For Aunt Edna'.[29]

Rattigan's next play did help to restore his reputation as a serious
dramatist. *Separate Tables* was another double-bill, set in a small
Bournemouth hotel. The first play develops Rattigan's familiar
themes of sexual longing and humiliation while the second pits a
man found guilty of interfering with women in a local cinema
against the self-appointed moral jurors in the hotel. The evening
was highly acclaimed and the subsequent Broadway production a
rare American success.

However, Rattigan's reign as the leading British playwright was
about to be brought to an abrupt end. In a car from Stratford to
London, early in 1956, Rattigan spent two and a half hours
informing his Oxford contemporary George Devine why the new
play he had discovered would not work in the theatre. When
Devine persisted, Rattigan answered 'Then I know nothing about
plays'. To which Devine replied, 'You know everything about
plays, but you don't know a fucking thing about *Look Back in
Anger.*' [30] Rattigan only barely attended the first night. He and
Hugh Beaumont wanted to leave at the interval until the critic T. C.
Worsley persuaded them to stay.[31]

The support for the English Stage Company's initiative was soon overwhelming. Osborne's play was acclaimed by the influential critics Kenneth Tynan and Harold Hobson, and the production was revived frequently at the Court, soon standing as the banner under which that disparate band of men (and women), the Angry Young Men, would assemble. Like many of his contemporaries, Rattigan decried the new movements, Beckett and Ionesco's turn from Naturalism, the wild invective of Osborne, the passionate socialism of Wesker, the increasing influence of Brecht. His opposition to them was perhaps intemperate, but he knew what was at stake: 'I may be prejudiced, but I'm pretty sure it won't survive,' he said in 1960, 'I'm prejudiced because if it *does* survive, I know I won't.' [32]

Such was the power and influence of the new movement that Rattigan almost immediately seemed old-fashioned. And from now on, his plays began to receive an almost automatic panning. His first play since *Separate Tables* (1954) was *Variation on a Theme* (1958). But between those dates the critical mood had changed. To make matters worse, there was the widely publicized story that nineteen year-old Shelagh Delaney had written the successful *A Taste of Honey* in two weeks after having seen *Variation on a Theme* and deciding that she could do better. A more sinister aspect of the response was the increasingly open accusation that Rattigan was dishonestly concealing a covert homosexual play within an apparently heterosexual one. The two champions of Osborne's play, Tynan and Hobson, were joined by Gerard Fay in the *Manchester Guardian* and Alan Brien in the *Spectator* to ask 'Are Things What They Seem?' [33]

When he is not being attacked for smuggling furtively homosexual themes into apparently straight plays, Rattigan is also criticized for lacking the courage to 'come clean' about his sexuality, both in his life and in his writing.[34] But neither of these criticisms really hit the mark. On the one hand, it is rather disingenuous to suggest that Rattigan should have 'come out'. The 1950s were a difficult time for homosexual men. The flight to the Soviet Union of Burgess and Maclean in 1951 sparked off a major witch-hunt against homosexuals, especially those in prominent positions. Cecil Beaton and Benjamin Britten were rumoured to be targets.[35] The police greatly stepped up the investigation and entrapment of homosexuals and prosecutions rose dramatically at the end of the forties, reaching a peak in 1953-54. One of their most infamous arrests for importuning, in October 1953, was that of John Gielgud.[36]

But neither is it quite correct to imply that somehow Rattigan's plays are *really* homosexual. This would be to misunderstand the way that homosexuality figured in the forties and early fifties. Wartime London saw a considerable expansion in the number of

pubs and bars where homosexual men (and women) could meet.
This network sustained a highly sophisticated system of gestural
and dress codes, words and phrases that could be used to indicate
one's sexual desires, many of them drawn from theatrical slang.
But the illegality of any homosexual activity ensured that these
codes could never become *too* explicit, *too* clear. Homosexuality,
then, was explored and experienced through a series of semi-
hidden, semi-open codes of behaviour; the image of the iceberg,
with the greater part of its bulk submerged beneath the surface, was
frequently employed.[37] And this image is, of course, one of the
metaphors often used to describe Rattigan's own playwriting.

Reaction came in the form of a widespread paranoia about the
apparent increase in homosexuality. The fifties saw a major drive to
seek out, understand, and often 'cure' homosexuality. The impetus
of these investigations was to bring the unspeakable and
underground activities of, famously, 'Evil Men' into the open, to
make it fully visible. The Wolfenden Report of 1957 was, without
doubt, a certain kind of liberalizing document in its recommen-
dation that consensual sex between adult men in private be
legalized. However the other side of its effect is to reinstate the
integrity of those boundaries – private/public, hidden/exposed,
homosexual/heterosexual – which homosexuality was broaching.
The criticisms of Rattigan are precisely part of this same desire to
divide, clarify and expose.

Many of Rattigan's plays were originally written with explicit
homosexual characters (*French Without Tears*, *The Deep Blue Sea*
and *Separate Tables*, for example), which he then changed.[38] But
many more of them hint at homosexual experiences and activities:
the relationship between Tony and David in *First Episode*, the
Major in *Follow my Leader* who is blackmailed over an incident
in Baghdad ('After all,' he explains, 'a chap's only human, and
it was a deuced hot night –'),[39] the suspiciously polymorphous
servicemen of *While the Sun Shines*, Alexander the Great and
T. E. Lawrence from *Adventure Story* and *Ross*, Mr Miller in
The Deep Blue Sea and several others. Furthermore, rumours of
Rattigan's own bachelor life circulated fairly widely. As indicated
above, Rattigan always placed great trust in the audiences of his
plays, and it was the audience which had to decode and reinterpret
these plays. His plays cannot be judged by the criterion of 'honesty'
and 'explicitness' that obsessed a generation after Osborne. They
are plays which negotiate sexual desire through structures of hint,
implications and metaphor. As David Rudkin has suggested, 'the
craftsmanship of which we hear so much loose talk seems to me
to arise from deep psychological necessity, a drive to organize the
energy that arises out of his own pain. Not to batten it down but to
invest it with some expressive clarity that speaks immediately to
people, yet keeps itself hidden'.[40]

The shifts in the dominant view of both homosexuality and
the theatre that took place in the fifties account for the brutal
decline of Rattigan's career. He continued writing, and while
Ross (1960) was reasonably well received, his ill-judged musical
adaptation of *French Without Tears*, *Joie de Vivre* (1960), was
a complete disaster, not assisted by a liberal bout of laryngitis
among the cast, and the unexpected insanity of the pianist.[41] It
ran for four performances.

During the sixties, Rattigan was himself dogged with ill-health:
pneumonia and hepatitis were followed by leukaemia. When his
death conspicuously failed to transpire, this last diagnosis was
admitted to be incorrect. Despite this, he continued to write,
producing the successful television play *Heart to Heart* in 1962,
and the stage play *Man and Boy* the following year, which received
the same sniping that greeted *Variation on a Theme*. In 1964, he
wrote *Nelson – a Portrait in Miniature* for Associated Television,
as part of a short season of his plays.

It was at this point that Rattigan decided to leave Britain and live
abroad. Partly this decision was taken for reasons of health; but
partly Rattigan just seemed no longer to be welcome. Ironically, it
was the same charge being levelled at Rattigan that he had faced in
the thirties, when the newspapers thundered against the those who
had supported the Oxford Union's pacifist motion as 'woolly-
minded Communists, practical jokers and sexual indeterminates'.[42]
As he confessed in an interview late in his life, 'Overnight almost,
we were told we were old-fashioned and effete and corrupt and
finished, and . . . I somehow accepted Tynan's verdict and went off
to Hollywood to write film scripts'.[43] In 1967 he moved to
Bermuda as a tax exile. A stage adaptation of his Nelson play, as
Bequest to the Nation, had a luke-warm reception.

Rattigan had a bad sixties, but his seventies seemed to indicate a
turnaround in his fortunes and reputation. At the end of 1970, a
successful production of *The Winslow Boy* was the first of ten years of
acclaimed revivals. In 1972, Hampstead Theatre revived *While the
Sun Shines* and a year later the Young Vic was praised for its *French
Without Tears*. In 1976 and 1977 *The Browning Version* was revived
at the King's Head and *Separate Tables* at the Apollo. Rattigan briefly
returned to Britain in 1971, pulled partly by his renewed fortune and
partly by the fact that he was given a knighthood in the New Year's
honours list. Another double bill followed in 1973: *In Praise of Love*
comprised the weak *Before Dawn* and the moving tale of emotional
concealment and creativity, *After Lydia*. Critical reception was more
respectful than usual, although the throwaway farce of the first play
detracted from the quality of the second.

Cause Célèbre, commissioned by BBC Radio and others,
concerned the Rattenbury case, in which Alma Rattenbury's aged

husband was beaten to death by her eighteen-year-old lover. Shortly after its radio première, Rattigan was diagnosed with bone cancer. Rattigan's response, having been through the false leukaemia scare in the early sixties, was to greet the news with unruffled elegance, welcoming the opportunity to 'work harder and indulge myself more'.[44] The hard work included a play about the Asquith family and a stage adaptation of *Cause Célèbre*, but, as production difficulties began to arise over the latter, the Asquith play slipped out of Rattigan's grasp. Although very ill, he returned to Britain, and on 4 July 1977, he was taken by limousine from his hospital bed to Her Majesty's Theatre, where he watched his last ever première. A fortnight later he had a car drive him around the West End where two of his plays were then running before boarding the plane for the last time. On 30 November 1977, in Bermuda, he died.

As Michael Billington's perceptive obituary noted, 'his whole work is a sustained assault on English middle class values: fear of emotional commitment, terror in the face of passion, apprehension about sex'.[45] In death, Rattigan began once again to be seen as someone critically opposed to the values with which he had so long been associated, a writer dramatizing dark moments of bleak compassion and aching desire.

Notes

1. Quoted in Rattigan's *Daily Telegraph* obituary (1 December 1977).

2. Michael Darlow and Gillian Hodson. *Terence Rattigan: The Man and His Work*. London and New York: Quartet Books, 1979, p. 26.

3. See, for example, Sheridan Morley. 'Terence Rattigan at 65.' *The Times*. (9 May 1977).

4. Terence Rattigan. Preface. *The Collected Plays of Terence Rattigan: Volume Two*. London: Hamish Hamilton, 1953, p. xv.

5. *Ibid.*, p. viii.

6. *Ibid.*, p. vii.

7. *Ibid.*, p. vii.

8. cf. Sheridan Morley, *op. cit.*

9. Humphrey Carpenter. *OUDS: A Centenary History of the Oxford University Dramatic Society*. With a Prologue by Robert Robinson. Oxford: Oxford University Press, 1985, p. 123.

10. Rattigan may well have reprised this later in life. John Osborne, in his autobiography, recalls a friend showing him a picture of Rattigan performing in an RAF drag show: 'He showed me a photograph of himself with Rattigan, dressed in a *tutu*, carrying a wand, accompanied by a line of aircraftsmen, during which Terry had sung his own show-stopper, "I'm just about the oldest fairy in the business. I'm quite the oldest fairy that you've ever seen".' John Osborne. *A Better Class of Person: An Autobiography, Volume I 1929-1956*. London: Faber and Faber, 1981, p. 223.

11. Darlow and Hodson *op. cit.*, p. 83.

12. Norman Gwatkin. Letter to Gilbert Miller, 28 July 1938. in: *Follow My Leader*. Lord Chamberlain's Correspondence: LR 1938. [British Library].

13. Richard Huggett. *Binkie Beaumont: Eminence Grise of the West Theatre 1933-1973*. London: Hodder & Stoughton, 1989, p. 308.

14. Terence Rattigan. Preface. *The Collected Plays of Terence Rattigan: Volume One*. London: Hamish Hamilton, 1953, p. xiv.

15. George Bernard Shaw, in: Keith Newman. *Two Hundred and Fifty Times I Saw a Play: or, Authors, Actors and Audiences*. With the facsimile of a comment by Bernard Shaw. Oxford: Pelagos Press, 1944, p. 2.

16. Henry Channon. *Chips: The Diaries of Sir Henry Channon*. Edited by Robert Rhodes James. Harmondsworth: Penguin, 1974, p. 480. Entry for 29 September 1944.

17. Tom Driberg. *Ruling Passions*. London: Jonathan Cape, 1977, p. 186.

18. See, for example, Norman Hart. 'Introducing Terence Rattigan,' *Theatre World*. xxxi, 171. (April 1939). p. 180 or Ruth Jordan. 'Another Adventure Story,' *Woman's Journal*. (August 1949), pp. 31-32.

19. Audrey Williamson. *Theatre of Two Decades*. New York and London: Macmillan, 1951, p. 100.

20. Terence Rattigan. 'Concerning the Play of Ideas,' *New Statesman and Nation*. (4 March 1950), pp. 241-242.

21. Terence Rattigan. 'The Play of Ideas,' *New Statesman and Nation* (13 May 1950), pp. 545-546. See also Susan Rusinko, 'Rattigan versus Shaw: The 'Drama of Ideas' Debate'. in: *Shaw: The Annual of Bernard Shaw Studies: Volume Two*. Edited by Stanley Weintraub. University Park, Penn: Pennsylvania State University Press, 1982. pp. 171-78.

22. John Elsom writes that Rattigan's plays 'represented establishment writing'. *Post-War British Drama*. Revised Edition. London: Routledge, 1979, p. 33.

23. B. A. Young. *The Rattigan Version: Sir Terence Rattigan and the Theatre of Character*. Hamish Hamilton: London, 1986, pp. 102-103; and Darlow and Hodson, *op. cit.*, p. 196, 204n.

24. Terence Rattigan. *Coll. Plays: Vol. Two. op. cit.*, pp. xi-xii.

25. *Ibid.*, p. xii.

26. *Ibid.*, p. xiv.

27. *Ibid.*, p. xvi.

28. *Ibid.*, p. xviii.

29. Opened on 17 September 1960. cf. *Plays and Players*. vii, 11 (November 1960).

30. Quoted in Irving Wardle. *The Theatres of George Devine*. London: Jonathan Cape, 1978, p. 180.

31. John Osborne. *Almost a Gentleman: An Autobiography, Volume II 1955-1966*. London: Faber and Faber, 1991, p. 20.

32. Robert Muller. 'Soul-Searching with Terence Rattigan.' *Daily Mail*. (30 April 1960).

33. The headline of Hobson's review in the *Sunday Times*, 11 May 1958.

34. See, for example, Nicholas de Jongh. *Not in Front of the Audience: Homosexuality on Stage*. London: Routledge, 1992, pp. 55-58.

35. Kathleen Tynan. *The Life of Kenneth Tynan*. Corrected Edition. London: Methuen, 1988, p. 118.

36. Cf. Jeffrey Weeks. *Coming Out: Homosexual Politics in Britain from the Nineteenth Century to the Present*. Revised and Updated Edition. London and New York: Quartet, 1990, p. 58; Peter Wildeblood. *Against the Law*. London: Weidenfeld and Nicolson, 1955, p. 46. The story of Gielgud's arrest may be found in Huggett, *op. cit.*, pp. 429-431. It was Gielgud's arrest which apparently inspired Rattigan to write the second part of *Separate Tables*, although again, thanks this time to the Lord Chamberlain, Rattigan had to change the Major's offence to a heterosexual one. See Darlow and Hodson, *op. cit.*, p. 228.

37. See, for example, Rodney Garland's novel about homosexual life in London, *The Heart in Exile*. London: W. H. Allen, 1953, p. 104.

38. See note 36; and also 'Rattigan Talks to John Simon,' *Theatre Arts*. 46 (April 1962), p. 24.

39. Terence Rattigan and Anthony Maurice. *Follow my Leader*. Typescript. Lord Chamberlain Play Collection: 1940/2. Box 2506. [British Library].

40. Quoted in Darlow and Hodson, *op. cit.,* p. 15.

41. B. A. Young, *op. cit.,* p. 162.

42. Quoted in Darlow and Hodson, *op. cit.,* p. 56.

43. Quoted in Sheridan Morley, *op. cit.*

44. Darlow and Hodson, *op. cit.,* p. 308.

45. *Guardian*. (2 December 1977).

The Browning Version & Harlequinade

In the late forties, Rattigan, like Strindberg fifty years before him, found himself watching with dismay the damage done to the flow and tension of a play by the imposition of an interval. So in the summer of 1948, Rattigan announced his intention to write four one-act plays which could be played in different, paired permutations through the course of a run.

His usual producer, Hugh 'Binkie' Beaumont of H. M. Tennent Ltd., was unenthusiastic, believing it impossible to attract audiences to this format.[1] In vain did Rattigan remind him that Coward's *Tonight at 8:30* had played successfully before the war, or that Olivier had scored a notable triumph with his double bill of *Oedipus* and *The Critic* at the Old Vic in 1945. The only way it could work, said Binkie, would be if John Gielgud were to agree to take the project on. Rattigan duly sent the plays to Gielgud, who was touring America with *The Importance of Being Earnest* and *Love for Love*. In October, Rattigan went out to meet him and, as they walked together in Central Park, Gielgud, notorious for his involuntary lapses in tact, delivered his verdict. "'I have to be so careful what I do now, Terry, my dear," he said. "The public have seen me in so much first-class stuff, do you think they would accept me in anything second-rate?"' [2] Although Gielgud later revised his opinion and played Andrew Crocker-Harris on radio and television, Rattigan was devastated and any hope of a Tennent production had to be abandoned. Casting around, Rattigan found Stephen Mitchell, who had had some success mounting Emlyn Williams's *The Corn is Green* before the war. He was now keen to produce a new play by the author of *French Without Tears* and *The Winslow Boy*.

Rattigan had written three of the projected four plays, but soon decided to fix upon two of them. *The Browning Version* and *Harlequinade* would play under the umbrella title, *Playbill*, both directed by his Oxford contemporary Peter Glenville, and starring Eric Portman and Mary Ellis. The third play, *High Summer*, was shelved until 1972, when Peter Duguid directed it for Thames Television.

The Browning Version gained Rattigan a second Ellen Terry Award for Best New Play, and Eric Portman's performance won Best Actor that season. Although it only ran for six months, *Playbill* has proved one of Rattigan's most popular and enduring works.

The Browning Version

As he often did, Rattigan drew on his personal experiences when writing his new play. When at Harrow, Rattigan had been taught classics by a Mr J. W. Coke-Norris, a harsh and humourless disciplinarian who had left Oxford, in his youth, with a rare double first. Rattigan was appalled by Norris's arid teaching of Aeschylus's *Agamemnon*, which saw it as purely a text from which to construe Greek, rather than to reconstruct theatrical experiences. When Norris retired, at the end of Rattigan's second year, one pupil (perhaps Rattigan himself) had given him a book as a leaving present, but had been rebuffed brusquely. Twenty years later, Rattigan called upon these memories to write his most acclaimed play yet.

Unanimously, the critics judged *The Browning Version* to have built most satisfyingly on the seriousness and power hinted at in some of the earlier works. Many critics noted the formal achievement of the play, praising the 'technical skill' (Cyril Ray, *Sunday Times*), and 'craftsmanship' (W. A. Darlington, *Daily Telegraph*).[3] Rattigan worked almost all of his life within the well-made play tradition, and he discussed its demands in an interview at the end of the sixties: 'A play isn't well made if you think about how well made it is, if you see the wheels turning'.[4] One of the great achievements of *The Browning Version* is the subtle choreography of incident such that we barely recognize the information being released to us or the manipulation of our emotional response. To pick one of many examples, early in the play Andrew Crocker-Harris shows Hunter the timetable he has designed. In less than a page of dialogue, we observe Crocker-Harris's fastidious pedantry, his anonymity within the school, Millie's open loathing of him, Crocker-Harris's acceptance of the decline in their marriage, and how little he will be missed when he has left. Rattigan constructs this short play around these moments, economically layering each event with a complex pattern of resonances and meanings. Rattigan's own 1951 film adaptation with Michael Redgrave as Crocker-Harris opened the play out; but by allowing characters to leave the play's one room, the dynamic economy of the writing was clouded.

But this much-vaunted technique was not simply for its own sake; the reviewer in the *Tatler and Bystander* remarked that the play was 'tragic and trivial, sentimental and poignant by turns, yet always acutely vivid' and the *Daily Mail* felt that 'one is looking in at the workings of real human souls'. But Harold Hobson's review in the *Sunday Times* was the most positive: 'as one listens wearily night after night to the banal, clipped, naturalistic dialogue of the modern drama,' he wrote, 'one's heart cries out for writing of courage and colour, for the evocative word and the bannered phrase. But Mr Rattigan makes one doubt the necessity of that cry'. He noted that while there is little dialogue in the play that reaches beyond the subdued Naturalism of the setting, Rattigan's fine drawing of the play's emotional life is such that by the end of the play the audience finds that 'its heart responds as to the sound of a trumpet'.

The subtle formal organization of the piece underpins a fast-flowing emotional current, nowhere better demonstrated than the extraordinary final sequence. Taplow returns to say goodbye to 'the Crock' and has brought him a small parting gift. This small kindness reduces Crocker-Harris to tears. The stumbling embarrassment of Taplow's explanation ('Verse translation of the *Agamemnon*, sir. The Browning version. It's not much good. I've been reading it in the chapel gardens.' p. 32)—is accentuated by the awkward pushing of the book to and fro between pupil and teacher, underscoring the exchange with a note of inarticulate awkwardness. But the full measure of Crocker-Harris's response is withheld from us. We see him read the inscription, wipe his glasses and replace them, brief pauses punctuating his speech, and then slowly his hands begin to shake. Much of the intensity of his long-forgotten emotion is left for the audience to infer since, even at this moment, he is careful to insist upon the correctness of Taplow's Greek diacritics: 'The perispomenon is perfectly correct' (p. 33). Crocker-Harris's collapse into tears is barely covered by his faltering explanation, and his sincere appreciation is insisted upon by his uncharacteristically repetitive discussion of Taplow's inscription.

Rattigan carefully prevents the scene from lapsing in sentiment, as it is this moment that Millie Crocker-Harris devastatingly punctures. Her cruel intervention, suggesting that the gift was nothing more than 'a few bobs' worth of appeasement' (p. 35), effects a sudden rise in the emotional temperature. It is now Hunter's turn to respond, and his bluff prosaic manner noticeably fails to match Millie's passionate intensity. As moving as Crocker-Harris's breakdown is the shift from Millie's callous dismissal of her husband ('Hurt? Andrew hurt? You can't hurt Andrew. He's dead.' p. 37) to her desperate and terrified attempts to preserve her affair with Hunter in the face of his inadequate passivity:

MILLIE. Frank, I don't care what humiliations you heap on me. I know you don't give two hoots for me as a person. I've always known that. I've never minded so long as you cared for me as a woman. And you do, Frank. You do. You do, don't you?

FRANK *is silent*.

It'll be all right in Bradford, you see. It'll be all right, there –

(p. 38)

This sudden shift of focus begins to set up the fine balance of emotions that is sustained until the end of the play.

During the fifties and sixties, Rattigan was unfashionable with the London critics (see my general introduction), although *The Browning Version* was frequently revived by regional repertory theatres and amateur groups, sometimes in the original double bill, as at the Sheffield Playhouse (1949) and Croydon Grand (1949), but more often on its own, with productions including those at the "Q" Theatre (1950), Golders Green Hippodrome (1957), Richmond Theatre (1960), Sheringham Little Theatre (1963), and Cheltenham Civic (1975).

The upswing in Rattigan's critical fortunes from the mid-seventies onwards prepared the way for a number of major revivals, that offered many opportunities to re-examine its subtle play of forces. One noticeable shift in perception has been of the rôle of Millie Crocker-Harris. The critics of the first production generally agreed with *The Sketch*'s verdict that 'there has not been this year a more hateful woman on our stage', and one described Mary Ellis's performance as 'a virulent piece of over-sexed nastiness'.[5] The first professional London revival in 1976 at the King's Head, Islington, directed by Stewart Potter, seemed to provoke similar feelings. Nigel Stock's Crocker-Harris was greatly praised, B. A. Young admiring the 'little explosions of passion that trouble, and once penetrate, the grey surfaces of his existence'.[6] However Barbara Jefford was felt to be hampered by a rôle which was 'just a bit too insensitive for real credibility'.[7] Nonetheless, the production was much admired and in July of that year the director, Stewart Potter, was awarded the Hugh Beaumont Award for Best Young Director outside the West End. Rattigan himself came to see the production, uneasy in the unfamiliar surroundings of a pub theatre, and astonished to find that the play was as well received in 1976 as it had been at the première.

In 1980, *The Browning Version* and *Harlequinade* were the first Rattigan plays to be performed at the National Theatre, featuring Alec McCowen as Crocker-Harris, Geraldine McEwan as Millie and Nicky Henson as Frank Hunter. But now critical perceptions had changed. According to B. A. Young, McEwan's Millie was 'never outwardly unpleasant, simply uttering her barbs of cruelty as if they were everyday conversation and so emphasising the sadness of having to live with them so long'.[8] For Michael Billington, McEwan 'rescues the wife from vulgar bitchery and shows her as someone equally trapped'.[9] And of Millie's cruellest moment Robert Cushman notes that 'Miss McEwan lets you see exactly why she does it'.[10] Only Sheridan Morley demurred, wishing McEwan had been the 'snobbish and vindictive wife' he felt Millie to be. Eight years later, at the Royalty Theatre in London's West End, Dorothy Tutin's Millie 'strides around the

stage with physically hungry savagery' her thwarted desires
only able to be released in the form of spite.[11] The play that *The
Browning Version* increasingly seems to be is not the sentimental
study of a failed teacher shackled to a vindictive wife, but an
examination of *two* people whose loves are different and whose
desires are incompatible. As Crocker-Harris says, 'You see, my
dear Hunter, she is really quite as much to be pitied as I' (p. 42).

The deceptions and ironies that run through the play constitute both
Rattigan's main concern and the dramatic principle around which
the text is constructed. From Taplow's calculated theft of one
chocolate rather than two, the play continually displays the
deliberate deceptions of its characters. They hide from each other,
put on acts for different audiences and ruthlessly attempt to pierce
each other's emotional armour. Millie plays at being the dutiful
schoolmaster's wife in front of the arch-diplomat Dr Frobisher,
whom she later describes as 'that old phoney of a headmaster'
(p. 25). And there is no mistaking the barbed irony of her remark to
Mrs Gilbert, 'Men have no souls, my dear. My husband is just as
bad' (p. 30). Boldly, Rattigan leaves open the possibility that
Taplow's gift may have been motivated in just the way Millie
describes and Crocker-Harris and Hunter both confess that they
play rôles in front of their pupils. In the rigidly formal world of an
English public school, it is the circulation of language, in the form
of nicknames, schoolboy gossip, an inscription in a book, or the
order of speeches at prize day that can make or mar a life.

Rattigan has been criticized for his lack of linguistic sophistication.[12] But here he gives every character a distinctive mode of
speaking, which gives each tiny moment of deviation particular
force. Crocker-Harris's first entrance soon establishes his quiet
pedantry: 'On the second day we managed to sell the seat to a
certain Dr. Lambert, who wore, I regret to say, the colours of the
opposing faction, but who otherwise seemed a passably agreeable
person' (p. 14); but when he recalls his youthful translation of the
Agamemnon, we hear the residues of a long-lost passion, strained
through the filters of an exhausted life: 'It was hard work; but I
derived great joy from it. The play had so excited and moved me
that I wished to communicate, however imperfectly, some of that
emotion to others. When I had finished it, I remember, I thought it
very beautiful — almost more beautiful than the original' (p. 18).
But now Aeschylus's play can do little more than provide him with
an uncomfortable echo of his own situation.

The final section of the play performs a delicate reversal of tone.
The war of attrition fought between husband and wife is
interrupted by Hunter's apparently earnest attempt to make contact
with Crocker-Harris. But now it is Hunter's long-perfected act, his
'false and hearty and jocular bonhomie' (p. 11), that traps him. His
aghast vision of the state of the Crocker-Harris marriage leads him

into fumbling hyperbole, 'No! That's too horrible to think of',
which Crocker-Harris firmly corrects: 'Nothing is ever too horrible
to think of, Hunter. It is simply a question of facing facts' (p. 40). It
is Hunter, often supposed to be Rattigan's voice in the play, who is
finally exposed as the ineffectual mediator, enslaved by an illusory
idealism, incapable of finding an appropriate response to the
despair he has witnessed.

The play ends on a magnificently fragile triangle of forces. Hunter
has failed to connect emotionally with Crocker-Harris, Millie's
affair is now over, and Crocker-Harris's momentary happiness has
been snatched from him. Rattigan gives us neither the simplicity of
a final closure (he resisted the tempting neatness of Crocker-
Harris's death from a heart-attack) nor the comfort of an optimistic
ending. For most of the play the Crocker-Harrises have dwelt upon
the past. It would be an exaggeration to say that the play ends with
them looking forward; but perhaps they are looking forward to
looking forward.

At the American première in 1949, *The Browning Version* was less
well received. The critics generally focused more closely on the
two stars, Maurice Evans and Edna Best, than on the plays, many
following Ward Morehouse's opinion in the *New York Sun* that the
plays were 'not particularly notable ... but they're turned into good
theater by showmanship and some superior performances'. The
New York Post agreed: 'both are highly effective vehicles for
acting'. The reviewer for the *New York Daily News* struck a popular
note when he dismissed the plays as being 'about a subject which
has an incomprehensible fascination for British playwrights – the
schoolmaster'.[13] However, not everyone was so disparaging and
much praise went to *The Browning Version*. The *New York Journal-
American* called it 'a masterpiece', the *New York Post* a 'striking,
thoughtful and sympathetic study', and the *New York Herald
Tribune* 'a new play of power and distinction'.[14] Rattigan was
moved by such criticism to speculate in an article for the *New York
Times* on the differences between British and American theatre, and
the 'sea-change' that affected British work when transferred across
the Atlantic.[15] However, performances of Britain's National Theatre
production of both parts of *Playbill* at the Baltimore International
Theatre Festival in June 1981 were acclaimed, and slowly New
York began to seem more attuned to Rattigan's work.[16]

However, in 1994, the play's persistent attractions were proven
with new film and stage productions. Clive Merrison played
Crocker-Harris to Diana Hardcastle's Millie in the Greenwich
Theatre production. Merrison allowed himself to become an
almost ludicrous figure, whose bookish mannerisms made
Hardcastle's frustrated rage entirely credible. The production
pointed up the links with the *Agamemnon*; and as Merrison's

Crocker-Harris underwent his collapse, as great sobs wracked his body in slow, almost graceful, spasms, lights behind a gauze briefly revealed Millie, dressed in white against a mountain background, suggesting both the Crocker-Harrises' first meeting in the Lake District and the play's classical antecedent. The play's enduring appeal was also shown in a second film treatment, starring Albert Finney, Greta Scacchi and Matthew Modine.

Rattigan apparently once suggested that if had 'to justify his choice of career before a heavenly jury, then *The Browning Version* would be the play he would want to represent him'.[17] Rattigan's great achievement in this play is to find the potential for such seriousness and clarity in what Crocker-Harris observes is 'usually, I believe, a subject for farce' (p. 42).

Harlequinade

In December 1939, the Committee for the Encouragement of Music and Arts (CEMA) was formed. Initially funded by a mixture of private donation (from the Pilgrim Trust) and the Ministry of Education, this body was entrusted to ensure that the collapse of cultural and artistic activity that took place during World War One was not repeated. In August 1946, this body was reconstituted as the Arts Council of Great Britain. The intermittent blackouts and curfews that beset London for much of the war meant that many commercial managements could only afford to maintain a profitable operation by touring, sometimes with CEMA's assistance, to venues outside London, many of which had rarely seen the slick, professional products in which theatrical managements like H. M. Tennent specialized. Other, somewhat more modest, operations also toured the country inspiring a wave of theatrical initiatives beyond the capital, the influence of which was continuing to be felt well into the seventies. Rattigan's *Harlequinade* dramatizes just such a touring outfit, and also reflects the acrimonious disputes within CEMA between those who wished to preserve the values of the West End and those who wished to use the theatre as a progressive force.

Another source for *Harlequinade* was Rattigan's experience working with the Lunts on his play *Love in Idleness*. Lynn Fontanne and Alfred Lunt were a famous husband-and-wife acting team. Their devotion to the theatre, as well as the curious discrepancies between their public image and private life provided Rattigan with inspiration for the Gosports and their touring production of *Romeo and Juliet,* which has arrived at a town in the Midlands. As one critic remarked of the Lunts, in terms which recall Jack the stage manager's own appraisal of the Gosports, they 'embody an elegance, a glossy frivolity of mind and heart, without which the art of the theatre in any society is felt to be drably incomplete'.[18] Later, Jack is asked whether the Gosports play husband and wife on stage. His answer is a shrewd analysis of the Lunts' appeal: 'No. Usually as a lover and a mistress. The audience prefers that — it gives them such a cosy feeling to know they're really married after all' (p. 64).

One final experience that fed into the writing of *Harlequinade* dates back to 1932, when Rattigan performed in the OUDS production of *Romeo and Juliet*. He had one line: 'Faith, we may put up our pipes and begone'. Rattigan put so much effort into the delivery of this line that he soon became quite unable to deliver it intelligibly. As a result, he spent the run mortified as each night he would be met with shouts of laughter. In *Harlequinade*, Rattigan has the First Halberdier offered the line when the old trouper George Chudleigh decides to retire just before opening night.

But many of the play's acutest and wittiest observations are drawn from Rattigan's own observations and experience of working in the theatre. Most of the players in the Gosports' company view the world through a proscenium arch. Arthur Gosport remembers the date 1926 because 'Gladys Cooper opened in *The Sign of the Door*' some moments before he can put his finger on the General Strike (p. 63). Later, he finds a baby in a pram left dangerously off-stage and is scandalized: 'It's very careless of people, leaving babies in the wings. There might be a very nasty accident. Somebody might easily trip over it and ruin their exit' (p. 65). Finally he discovers that the baby is his grandson; appraising its appearance, he notes, 'It looks—(*with a sob*)—like Beerbohm Tree' (p. 77).

Harlequinade is an undemanding but enjoyable farce. It is perhaps marred by an indeterminacy of focus as the shrewdly-observed satire occasionally gives way to sentimental paeans to the joys of theatre folk and as the one-liners begin to compete with, rather than complement, the rather clumsy paternity farce that develops halfway through. But the play introduces a number of wonderful creations: Edna Selby and Arthur Gosport's absurd vanity which demands that, in an attempt to hide their unsuitability as teenage lovers, they turn the stage lights so low that they fuse; Arthur's mother, Dame Maud Gosport whose increasingly irritating acting tips and nostalgic recollections punctuate the rehearsal; and the calmly efficient stage manager, Jack, who knows how to solve any problem, except how to tell these great actors that he wants to leave the theatre and marry his fiancée.

Some of Rattigan's side-swipes at the contemporary theatre have dated. The late forties saw a huge upsurge of poetic drama, with plays by T. S. Eliot, Christopher Fry and Ronald Duncan all achieving successful West End runs. The latter's *This Way to the Tomb* is obliquely hinted at in the title of the poetic drama planned for the Gosports' East European tour, *Follow the Leviathan to My Father's Grave*. But some of the jabs at the Arts Council are wittily judged to deflate the fledging organization's zeal for social engineering.

EDNA: ... The theatre of today has at last acquired a social conscience and a social purpose...

DAME MAUD: Oh, I didn't know it was social purpose that brought us here. I thought it was CEMA.

EDNA: CEMA is social purpose.

DAME MAUD: Is it, dear? Fancy! (p. 56)

At times, Rattigan's wit deserts him and his view of the new arts funding becomes rather sermonizing. But perhaps this is not surprising; the West End managements, with which Rattigan had scored his major success, were disdainful of the concessions they were having to make to CEMA, and especially its crusading founder-member, Lewis Casson. After a slightly worthy season of classic British plays, Binkie Beaumont is reported as saying: "'At least Lewis liked it; he'll probably want us to take it round the Welsh mining villages. Can you *imagine?*" ' [19]

The critics were divided on *Harlequinade*. Many were accepting of its modest pretensions: 'a refreshing romp,' decided the *Tatler and Bystander*, and the *Daily Telegraph* took it as 'a delicious skit'. On its 1980 revival, many were surprised by how fresh the play still seemed, and Nicky Henson was praised for his transformation of Jack into a virtuoso comic part. In 1988, when the order of the two plays was reversed and *Harlequinade* played first, Peter Kemp noted the powerful effect of seeing Eddington's expansive Arthur Gosport cramped into the stiff bodily reserve of Andrew Crocker-Harris after the interval. In America, where not even *The Browning Version* had received unalloyed praise, the comedy was dismissed as 'a slight and overwritten comedy' (*New York Herald Tribune*) and 'a pretty embarrassing escapade' (*New York Times*).

However, the power and poise of *The Browning Version* neatly balanced the frivolity of *Harlequinade*. And by the end of the 1940s, it seemed as though Rattigan's dreams of being considered a serious writer were on the brink of being realized.

DAN REBELLATO

Notes

I would like to thank the staff of the Theatre Museum, London, for their help in tracing revivals and reviews of *The Browning Version* and *Harlequinade*.

1. Beaumont would later make the same mistake with *Separate Tables* in 1954.

2. Richard Huggett. *Binkie Beaumont: Eminence Grise of the West Theatre 1933-1973.* London: Hodder & Stoughton, 1989, p. 401. Some have suggested that this story may have been exaggerated by Rattigan, stung by Gielgud's refusal.

3. British review comments, if unattributed, are drawn from B. A. Young. *The Rattigan Version: Sir Terence Rattigan and the Theatre of Character.* Hamish Hamilton: London, 1986, p. 79, or the Production File for *Playbill.* Phoenix Theatre. 8 September 1948, in the Theatre Museum, London.

4. An interview with Irma Kurtz for *Nova* (March 1967), pp. 60-63.

5. *The Sketch,* 29 September 1948; Audrey Williamson. *Theatre of Two Decades.* New York and London: Macmillan, 1951, p. 102.

6. *Financial Times*, 9 January 1976.

7. *Evening Standard*, 12 January 1976.

8. *Financial Times,* 15 May 1980.

9. *The Guardian*, 15 May 1980.

10. *The Observer*, 18 May 1980.

11. *Independent*, 19 March 1988.

12. See, for example, B. A. Young. Preface in: *The Collected Plays of Terence Rattigan: Volume Four.* London: Hamish Hamilton, 1978.

13. Since John Van Druten's *Young Woodley* (1928), and especially in the forties, a string of British plays had tried to dramatize aspects of school life: Reginald Beckwith's *Boys in Brown* (1940), Warren Chetham-Strode's *The Guinea Pig* (1946), Robert Morley and Noel Langley's *Edward, My Son* and Travers Otway's *The Hidden Years* (1947) being among the best known.

14. This and other American reviews quoted from *New York Critics' Reviews*. x, 22 (17 October 1949), pp. 253-257.

15. B. A. Young, *The Rattigan Version, op. cit.,* p. 78.

16. cf. Holly Hill. 'Rattigan's Renaissance.' *Contemporary Review*. ccxxxx, 1392. (January 1982). pp. 37-42.

17. Michael Darlow and Gillian Hodson. *Terence Rattigan: The Man and His Work*. London and New York: Quartet Books, 1979, p. 167.

18. Laurence Kitchin. *Mid-Century Drama*. Revised Edition. London: Faber and Faber, 1962, p. 204.

19. Richard Huggett. *op. cit.,* p. 305.

List of Rattigan's Produced Plays

TITLE	BRITISH PREMIERE	NEW YORK PREMIERE
First Episode (with Philip Heimann)	Q Theatre, Kew, 11 Sept 1933 (transferred to Comedy Theatre, 26 Jan 1934	Ritz Theatre, 17 Sept 1934
French Without Tears	Criterion Theatre, 6 Nov 1936	Henry Miller Theatre, 28 Sept 1937
After the Dance	St James's Theatre, 21 June 1939	
Follow My Leader (with Anthony Maurice, alias Tony Goldschmidt)	Apollo Theatre, 16 Jan 1940	
Grey Farm (with Hector Bolitho)		Hudson Theatre, 3 May 1940
Flare Path	Apollo Theatre, 13 Aug 1932	Henry Miller Theatre, 23 Dec 1942
While the Sun Shines	Globe Theatre, 24 Dec 1943	Lyceum Theatre, 19 Sept 1944
Love in Idleness	Lyric Theatre, 20 Dec 1944	Empire Theatre (as *O Mistress Mine*), 23 Jan 1946
The Winslow Boy	Lyric Theatre, 23 May 1946	Empire Theatre, 29 Oct 1947
Playbill (*The Browning Version* and *Harlequinade*)	Phoenix Theatre, 8 Sept 1948	Coronet Theatre, 12 Oct 1949
Adventure Story	St James's Theatre, 17 March 1949	
A Tale of Two Cities (from Charles Dickens, with John Gielgud)	St Brendan's College Dramatic Society, Clifton, 23 Jan 1950	
Who is Sylvia?	Criterion Theatre, 24 Oct 1950	
Final Test (TV)	BBC TV, 29 July 1951	

The Deep Blue Sea	Duchess Theatre, 6 Mar 1952	Morosco Theatre, 5 Nov 1952
The Sleeping Prince	Phoenix Theatre, 5 Nov 1953	Coronet Theatre, 1 Nov 1956
Seperate Tables (*The Table by the Window* and *Table Number Seven*)	St James's Theatre, 22 Sept 1954	Music Box Theatre, 25 Oct 1956
Variation on a Theme	Globe Theatre, 8 May 1958	
Ross	Theatre Royal Haymarket 12 May 1960	Eugene O'Neill Theatre 26 Dec 1961
Joie de Vivre (with Robert Stolz and Paul Dehn)	Queen's Theatre, 14 July 1960	
Heart to Heart (TV)	BBC TV, 6 Dec 1962	
Man and Boy	Queen's Theatre, 4 Sept 1963	Brooks Atkinson Theatre, 12 Nov 1963
Ninety Years On (TV)	BBC TV, 29 Nov 1964	
Nelson – A Portrait in Miniature (TV)	Associated Television, 21 Mar 1966	
All On Her Own (TV) (adapted for the stage as *Duologue*)	BBC 2, 25 Sept 1968	
A Bequest to the Nation	Theatre Royal Haymarket 23 Sept 1970	
High Summer (TV)	Thames TV, 12 Sept 1972	
In Praise of Love (*After Lydia* and *Before Dawn*)	Duchess Theatre, 27 Sept 1973	Morosco Theatre, 10 Dec 1974
Cause Célèbre (radio)	BBC Radio 4, 27 Oct 1975	
Duologue	King's Head Theatre, 21 Feb 1976	
Cause Célèbre (stage)	Her Majesty's Theatre, 4 July 1977	
Less Than Kind	Jermyn Street Theatre, 20 January 2011	

THE BROWNING VERSION

Characters

JOHN TAPLOW
FRANK HUNTER
MILLIE CROCKER-HARRIS
ANDREW CROCKER-HARRIS
DR. FROBISHER
PETER GILBERT
MRS. GILBERT

Scene: *the sitting-room of the Crocker Harrises' rooms in a public school in the South of England.*

The Browning Version was first produced in a double-bill with *Harlequinade* under the joint title, *Playbill*, at the Phoenix Theatre, London, on September 8th, 1948, with the following cast:

JOHN TAPLOW	Peter Scott
FRANK HUNTER	Hector Ross
MILLIE CROCKER-HARRIS	Mary Ellis
ANDREW CROCKER-HARRIS	Campbell Cotts
DR. FROBISHER	Eric Portman
PETER GILBERT	Anthony Oliver
MRS. GILBERT	Henryetta Edwards

The play directed by PETER GLENVILLE

The Browning Version

Scene: the sitting-room of the Crocker-Harrises' rooms in a public school in the South of England. It is between six and seven o'clock on a July evening. The building in which the rooms are situated is large and Victorian, and at some fairly recent date has been converted into flats of varying size for masters, married and unmarried. The Crocker-Harrises have the ground floor and their sitting-room is probably the biggest – and gloomiest – room in the house. It boasts, however, access (through a stained-glass door, L.) to a small garden, and is furnished with chintzy and genteel cheerfulness. Another door, back R., leads into the hall and the rest of the flat. This door is concealed by a screen.

The room is empty at the rise of the curtain, but we hear the front door opening and closing and, immediately after, a timorous knock on the door, repeated after a pause.

Finally the door opens and JOHN TAPLOW *makes his appearance. He is a plain, moon-faced boy of about sixteen, with glasses. He stands in doubt at the door for a moment, then goes back into the hall, where we hear him calling.*

TAPLOW. (*Calling off.*) Sir! Sir!

> *After a pause, he re-enters. He is dressed in grey flannels, a dark blue coat, and white scarf. He goes to the garden door and opens it.*

(*Calling.*) Sir!

> *There is no reply.* TAPLOW, *standing in the bright sunshine at the door, emits a plaintive sigh, then closes it firmly and goes to a table on which he places a book, a notebook, and a pen.*

> *On the table is a small box of chocolates, probably the Crocker-Harrises' ration for the month.* TAPLOW *opens the box, counts the number inside, and removes two. One of these he eats and the other, after a second's struggle, either with his conscience or his judgment of what he might be able to get away with, he virtuously replaces in the box. Finally he picks up a walking-stick with a crooked handle and makes a couple of golf swings, with an air of great concentration.*

> FRANK HUNTER *appears from behind the screen covering the door. He is a rugged young man – not perhaps quite as rugged as his deliberately-cultivated manner of ruthless honesty makes him appear, but wrapped in all the self-confidence of the*

popular master. He watches TAPLOW, *whose back is to the door, making his swing.*

FRANK. Roll the wrists away from the ball. Don't break them like that.

He walks over quickly and puts his large hands over the abashed TAPLOWS.

Now swing.

TAPLOW, *guided by* FRANK'S *evidently expert hands, succeeds in hitting the carpet with more effect than before.*

Too quick. Slow back and stiff left arm. It's no good just whacking the ball as if you were the headmaster and the ball was you. It'll never go more than fifty yards if you do. Get a rhythm. A good golf swing is a matter of aesthetics, not of brute strength.

TAPLOW, *only half-listening, is gazing at the carpet.*

FRANK. What's the matter?

TAPLOW. I think we've made a tear in the carpet, sir.

FRANK *examines the carpet perfunctorily.*

FRANK. Nonsense. That was there already. (*He puts the stick in a corner of the room.*) Do I know you?

TAPLOW. No, sir.

FRANK. What's your name?

TAPLOW. Taplow.

FRANK. Taplow! No, I don't. You're not a scientist I gather?

TAPLOW. No, sir. I'm still in the lower fifth. I can't specialize until next term – that's to say if I've got my remove all right.

FRANK. Don't you know yet if you've got your remove?

TAPLOW. No, sir. Mr. Crocker-Harris doesn't tell us the results like the other masters.

FRANK. Why not?

TAPLOW. Well, you know what he's like, sir.

FRANK. I believe there is a rule that form results should only be announced by the headmaster on the last day of term.

TAPLOW. Yes – but who else pays any attention to it – except Mr. Crocker-Harris?

FRANK. I don't, I admit – but that's no criterion. So you've got to wait until tomorrow to know your fate, have you?

TAPLOW. Yes, sir.

FRANK. Supposing the answer is favourable – what then?

TAPLOW. Oh – science, sir, of course.

FRANK. (*Sadly.*) Yes. We get all the slackers.

TAPLOW. (*Protestingly.*) I'm extremely interested in science, sir.

FRANK. Are you? I'm not. Not at least in the science I have to teach.

TAPLOW. Well, anyway, sir, it's a good deal more exciting than this muck. (*Indicating his book.*)

FRANK. What is this muck?

TAPLOW. Aeschylus, sir. The *Agamemnon*.

FRANK. And your considered view is that the *Agamemnon* of Aeschylus is muck, is it?

TAPLOW. Well, no, sir. I don't think the play is muck – exactly. I suppose, in a way, it's rather a good plot, really, a wife murdering her husband and having a lover and all that. I only meant the way it's taught to us – just a lot of Greek words strung together and fifty lines if you get them wrong.

FRANK. You sound a little bitter, Taplow.

TAPLOW. I am rather, sir.

FRANK. Kept in, eh?

TAPLOW. No, sir. Extra work.

FRANK. Extra work – on the last day of school?

TAPLOW. Yes, sir – and I might be playing golf. You'd think *he'd* have enough to do anyway himself, considering he's leaving tomorrow for good – but oh no. I missed a day last week when I had 'flu – so here I am – and look at the weather, sir.

FRANK. Bad luck. Still, there's one consolation. You're pretty well bound to get your remove tomorrow for being a good boy in taking extra work.

TAPLOW. Well, I'm not so sure, sir. That would be true of the ordinary masters, all right. They just wouldn't dare not give a chap a remove after his taking extra work – it would be such a bad advertisement for them. But those sort of rules don't apply to the Crock – Mr. Crocker-Harris. I asked him yesterday outright if he'd given me a remove and do you know what he said, sir?

FRANK. No. What?

TAPLOW. (*Mimicking a very gentle, rather throaty voice*.) 'My dear Taplow, I have given you exactly what you deserve. No less; and certainly no more.' Do you know, sir, I think he may have marked me down, rather than up, for taking extra work. I mean, the man's barely human. (*He breaks off quickly*.) Sorry, sir. Have I gone too far?

FRANK. Yes. Much too far.

TAPLOW. Sorry, sir. I got sort of carried away.

FRANK. Evidently. (*He picks up* The Times *and opens it*.) Er – Taplow.

TAPLOW. Yes, sir?

FRANK. What was that Mr. Crocker-Harris said to you? Just – er – repeat it, would you?

TAPLOW. (*Mimicking again*.) 'My dear Taplow, I have given you exactly what you deserve. No less; and certainly no more.'

FRANK *snorts, then looks stern*.

FRANK. Not in the least like him. Read your nice Aeschylus and be quiet.

TAPLOW. (*With weary disgust*.) Aeschylus.

FRANK. Look, what time did Mr. Crocker-Harris tell you to be here?

TAPLOW. Six-thirty, sir.

FRANK. Well, he's ten minutes late. Why don't you cut? You could still get nine holes in before lock-up.

TAPLOW. (*Genuinely shocked*.) Oh, no, I couldn't cut. Cut the Crock – Mr. Crocker-Harris? I shouldn't think it's ever been done in the whole time he's been here. God knows what would happen if I did. He'd probably follow me home, or something –

FRANK. I must admit I envy him the effect he seems to have on you boys in his form. You all seem scared to death of him. What does he do – beat you all, or something?

TAPLOW. Good lord, no. He's not a sadist, like one or two of the others.

FRANK. I beg your pardon?

TAPLOW. A sadist, sir, is someone who gets pleasure out of giving pain.

FRANK. Indeed? But I think you went on to say that some other masters –

TAPLOW. Well, of course they are, sir. I won't mention names, but you know them as well as I do. Of course I know most masters think we boys don't understand a thing – but dash it, sir, you're different. You're young – well comparatively anyway – and you're science and you canvassed for Labour in the last election. You must know what sadism is.

FRANK. (*After a pause.*) Good lord! What are public schools coming to?

TAPLOW. Anyway the Crock isn't a sadist. That's what I'm saying. He wouldn't be so frightening if he were – because at least it would show he had some feelings. But he hasn't. He's all shrivelled up inside like a nut and he seems to hate people to like him. It's funny, that. I don't know any other master who doesn't like being liked –

FRANK. And I don't know any boy who doesn't trade on that very foible.

TAPLOW. Well, it's natural, sir. But not with the Crock –

FRANK. (*Making a feeble attempt at re-establishing the correct relationship.*) Mr. Crocker-Harris.

TAPLOW. Mr. Crocker-Harris. The funny thing is that in spite of everything, I do rather like him. I can't help it. And sometimes I think he sees it and that seems to shrivel him up even more –

FRANK. I'm sure you're exaggerating.

TAPLOW. No, sir. I'm not. In form the other day he made one of his little classical jokes. Of course nobody laughed because nobody understood it, myself included. Still, I knew he'd meant it as funny, so I laughed. Not out of sucking-up, sir, I swear, but ordinary common politeness, and feeling a bit sorry for him having made a dud joke. (*He goes to the table and sits down.*) Now I can't remember what the joke was – but let's say it was (*adopting his imitative voice again.*) benedictus, benedicatur, benedictine . . . Now, you laugh, sir –

FRANK *laughs.* TAPLOW *looks at him over an imaginary pair of spectacles, and then, very gently, crooks his forefinger to him in indication to approach the table.* FRANK *does so – simply, not clowning. He is genuinely interested in the incident.*

(*In a gentle, throaty voice.*). 'Taplow – you laughed at my little pun, I noticed. I must confess I am flattered at the evident advance your Latinity has made that you should so readily have understood what the rest of the form did not. Perhaps, now, you would be good enough to explain it to them, so that they too can share your pleasure.'

The door behind the screen is pushed open and MILLIE
CROCKER-HARRIS *appears. She is a thin woman in the late
thirties, rather more smartly dressed than the general run of
schoolmasters' wives. She stands by the screen pulling off her
gloves and watching* TAPLOW *and* FRANK. *It is a few seconds
before they notice her.*

'Come along, Taplow. Do not be so selfish as to keep a good
joke to yourself. Tell the others – ' (*He breaks off suddenly,
seeing* MILLIE.) Oh lord!

FRANK *turns quickly, and seems infinitely relieved at seeing*
MILLIE.

FRANK. Oh, hullo.

MILLIE. (*Without expression.*) Hullo.

*She puts down a couple of parcels she has been carrying, and
goes back into the hall to take off her hat.*

TAPLOW. (*Frantically whispering to* FRANK.) Do you think she
heard?

FRANK *shakes his head comfortably.*

I think she did. She was standing there quite a time. If she did
and she tells him, there goes my remove –

FRANK. Nonsense –

MILLIE *comes back into the room.*

MILLIE. (*To* TAPLOW.) Waiting for my husband?

TAPLOW. Er – yes.

MILLIE. He's at the Bursar's and might be there quite a time. If I
were you I'd go.

TAPLOW. (*Doubtfully.*) He said most particularly I was to come –

MILLIE. Well? why don't you run away for a quarter of an hour
and come back?

TAPLOW. Supposing he gets here before me?

MILLIE. (*Smiling.*) I'll take the blame. I tell you what – you can do
a job for him. Take this prescription to the chemist and get it
made up.

TAPLOW. All right, Mrs. Crocker-Harris.

MILLIE. And while you're there you might as well slip into
Stewarts and have an ice. Here. Catch. (*She takes a shilling from
her bag and throws it to him.*)

TAPLOW. Thanks awfully. (*He passes* FRANK *on his way to the door. In a whisper.*) See she doesn't tell him.

FRANK. O.K.

MILLIE. (*Turning as* TAPLOW *is going.*) Oh, Taplow –

TAPLOW. Yes, Mrs. Crocker-Harris.

MILLIE. I had a letter from my father today in which he says he once had the pleasure of meeting your mother –

TAPLOW. (*Uninterested, but polite.*) Oh, really?

MILLIE. Yes. It was at some fête or other in Bradford. My uncle – that's Sir William Bartop, you know – made a speech and so did your mother. My father met her afterwards at tea –

TAPLOW. Oh, really?

MILLIE. He said he found her quite charming.

TAPLOW. Yes, she's jolly good at those sort of functions. (*Aware of his lack of tact.*) I mean – I'm sure she found him charming, too. Well – I'd better get going. So long.

TAPLOW *goes out.*

MILLIE. Thank you for coming round.

FRANK. That's all right.

MILLIE. You're staying for dinner?

FRANK. If I may.

MILLIE. If you may! Give me a cigarette.

He extends his case. She takes a cigarette.

(*Indicating case.*) You haven't given it away yet, I see.

FRANK. Do you think I would?

MILLIE. Frankly, yes. Luckily it's a man's case. I don't suppose any of your girl friends would want it –

FRANK. Don't be silly.

MILLIE. Where have you been all this week?

FRANK. Correcting exam papers – making reports. You know what end of term is like –

MILLIE. I do know what end of term is like. But even Andrew has managed this last week to take a few hours off to say goodbye to people –

FRANK. I really have been appallingly busy. Besides I'm coming to stay with you in Bradford –

MILLIE. Not for over a month. Andrew doesn't start his new job until September first. That's one of the things I had to tell you.

FRANK. Oh, I had meant to be in Devonshire in September.

MILLIE. (*Quickly.*) Who with?

FRANK. My family.

MILLIE. Surely you can go earlier, can't you? Go in August.

FRANK. It'll be difficult.

MILLIE. Then you'd better come to me in August.

FRANK. But Andrew will still be there.

MILLIE. Yes.

Pause.

FRANK. I think I can manage September.

MILLIE. That'd be better – from every point of view. Except that it means I shan't see you for six weeks.

FRANK. (*Lightly.*) You'll survive that, all right.

MILLIE. Yes, I'll survive it – but not as easily as you will.

FRANK *says nothing*.

I haven't much pride, have I? (*She approaches him.*) Frank, darling, I love you so much –

He kisses her, on the mouth, but a trifle perfunctorily, and then breaks quickly away, as if afraid someone had come into the room.

(*Laughing.*) You're very nervous.

FRANK. I'm afraid of that screen arrangement. You can't see people coming in –

MILLIE. Oh, yes. That reminds me. What were you and Taplow up to when I came in just now? Making fun of my husband?

FRANK. Afraid so. Yes.

MILLIE. It sounded rather a good imitation. I must get him to do it for me some time. It was very naughty of you to encourage him.

FRANK. I know. It was.

MILLIE. (*Ironically.*) Bad for discipline.

FRANK. Exactly. Currying favour with the boys, too. My God, how easy it is to be popular. I've only been a master three years but I've already slipped into an act and a vernacular that I just can't get out of. Why can't anyone ever be natural with the little blighters?

MILLIE. They probably wouldn't like it if you were.

FRANK. I don't see why not. No one seems to have tried it yet, anyway. I suppose the trouble is – we're all too scared of them. Either one gets forced into an attitude of false and hearty and jocular bonhomie like myself, or into the sort of petty, soulless tyranny which your husband uses to protect himself against the lower fifth.

MILLIE. (*Rather bored with this.*) He'd never be popular whatever he did –

FRANK. Possibly not. He ought never to have become a schoolmaster, really. Why did he?

MILLIE. It was his vocation, he said. He was sure he'd make a big success of it, especially when he got his job here first go *off*. (*Bitterly.*) Fine success he's made, hasn't he?

FRANK. You should have stopped him.

MILLIE. How was I to know? He talked about getting a house, then a headmastership.

FRANK. The Crock a headmaster! That's a pretty thought.

MILLIE. Yes, it's funny to think of it now, all right. Still he wasn't always the Crock, you know. He had a bit more gumption once. At least I thought he had. Don't let's talk any more about him – it's too depressing.

FRANK. I'm sorry for him.

MILLIE. (*Indifferently.*) He's not sorry for himself, so why should you be? It's me you should be sorry for.

FRANK. I am.

MILLIE. (*Smiling.*) Then show me.

She stretches out her arms to him. He kisses her again quickly and lightly, but she holds him hungrily. He has to free himself almost roughly.

FRANK. What have you been doing all day?

MILLIE. Calling on the other masters' wives – saying fond farewells. I've worked off twelve. I've another seven to do tomorrow.

FRANK. You poor thing! I don't envy you.

MILLIE. It's the housemasters' wives that are the worst. They're all so damn patronizing. You should have heard Betty Carstairs. 'My dear – it's such terrible bad luck on you both – that your husband should get this heart trouble just when, if only he'd stayed on, he'd have been bound to get a house. I mean, he's considerably senior to my Arthur as it is, and they simply couldn't have gone on passing him over, could they?'

FRANK. There's a word for Betty Carstairs, my dear, that I would hesitate to employ before a lady.

MILLIE. She's got her eye on you, anyway.

FRANK. Betty Carstairs? What utter rot!

MILLIE. Oh, yes, she has. I saw you at that concert. Don't think I didn't notice.

FRANK. Millie, darling! Really! I detest the woman.

MILLIE. Then what were you doing in her box at Lord's?

FRANK. Carstairs invited me. I went there because it was a good place to see the match from.

MILLIE. Yes, I'm sure it was. Much better than the grandstand, anyway.

FRANK. (*As if remembering something suddenly.*) Oh, my God!

MILLIE. It's all right, my dear. Don't bother to apologize. We gave the seat away, as it happens –

FRANK. I'm most terribly sorry.

MILLIE It's all right. We couldn't afford a box, you see –

FRANK. It wasn't that. You know it wasn't that. It's just that I – well, I clean forgot.

MILLIE. Funny you didn't forget the Carstairs's invitation –

FRANK. Millie – don't be a fool.

MILLIE. It's you who are the fool. (*Appealingly.*) Frank – have you never been in love? I know you're not in love with me – but haven't you ever been in love with anyone? Don't you realize what torture you inflict on someone who loves you when you do a thing like that?

FRANK. I've told you I'm sorry – I don't know what more I can say.

MILLIE. Why not the truth?

FRANK. The truth is – I clean forgot.

MILLIE. The truth is – you had something better to do – and why not say it?

FRANK. All right. Believe that if you like. It happens to be a lie, but believe it all the same. Only for God's sake stop this –

MILLIE. Then for God's sake show me some pity. Do you think it's any pleasanter for me to believe that you cut me because you forgot? Do you think that doesn't hurt either?

FRANK *turns away.*

Oh, damn! I was so determined to be brave and not mention Lord's. Why did I? Frank, just tell me one thing. Just tell me you're not running away from me – that's all I want to hear.

FRANK. I'm coming to Bradford.

MILLIE. I think, if you don't, I'll kill myself.

FRANK. I'm coming to Bradford.

The door is pushed open. FRANK *has made a move towards* MILLIE *but stops at the sound.* MILLIE *has recovered herself as* ANDREW CROCKER-HARRIS *appears by the screen. Despite the summer sun he wears a serge suit and a stiff collar. He carries a portfolio and looks, as ever, neat, complacent, and unruffled. He speaks in a very gentle voice which he rarely raises.*

ANDREW. Is Taplow here?

MILLIE. I sent him to the chemist to get your prescription made up –

ANDREW. What prescription?

MILLIE. Your heart medicine. Don't you remember? You told me this morning it had run out –

ANDREW. Of course I remember, my dear, but there was no need to send Taplow for it. If you had telephoned the chemist he would have sent it round in plenty of time. He knows the prescription. Now Taplow will be late and I am so pressed for time I hardly know how to fit him in.

This colloquy has taken place near the door, the screen and MILLIE, *blocking* ANDREW'S *view of the room. As he now comes in he sees* FRANK.

Ah, Hunter! How are you?

FRANK. Very well, thanks.

They shake hands.

ANDREW. Most kind of you to drop in, but, as Millie should have warned you, I am expecting a pupil for extra work and –

MILLIE. He's staying to dinner, Andrew.

ANDREW. Good. Then I shall see something of you. However, when Taplow returns I'm sure you won't mind –

FRANK. (*Making a move.*) No, of course not. I'll make myself scarce now, if you'd rather – I mean, if you're busy –

ANDREW. Oh, no. There is no need for that. Sit down, do. Will you smoke? I don't, as you know, but Millie does. Millie, give our guest a cigarette –

MILLIE. I haven't any, I'm afraid. I've had to cadge from him.

FRANK *takes out his cigarette case and offers it to* MILLIE *who exchanges a glance with him as she takes one.*

ANDREW. We expected you at Lord's, Hunter.

FRANK. What? Oh, yes. I'm most terribly sorry. I –

MILLIE. He clean forgot, Andrew. Imagine.

ANDREW. Forgot?

MILLIE. Not everyone is blessed with your superhuman memory, you see.

FRANK. I really can't apologize enough –

ANDREW. Please don't bother to mention it. On the second day we managed to sell the seat to a certain Dr. Lambert, who wore, I regret to say, the colours of the opposing faction, but who otherwise seemed a passably agreeable person. You liked him, didn't you, Millie?

MILLIE. (*Looking at* FRANK.) Very much, indeed. I thought him quite charming.

ANDREW. A charming old gentleman. (*To* FRANK.) You have had tea?

FRANK. Yes – thank you –

ANDREW. Is there any other refreshment I can offer you?

FRANK. No, thank you.

ANDREW. Would it interest you to see the new timetable I have drafted for next term?

FRANK. Yes, very much.

ANDREW *has taken out a long roll of paper, made by pasting pieces of foolscap together and which is entirely covered by his meticulous writing.*

I never knew you drafted our timetables –

ANDREW. Didn't you? I have done so for the last fifteen years. Of course they are always issued in mimeograph under the headmaster's signature – Now what form do you take? upper fifth Science – there you are – that's the general picture, but on the back you will see each form specified under separate headings – there – that's a new idea of mine – Millie, this might interest you –

MILLIE. (*Suddenly harsh.*) You know it bores me to death –

FRANK *looks up, surprised and uncomfortable.* ANDREW *does not remove his eyes from the timetable.*

ANDREW. Millie has no head for this sort of work. There you see. Now here you can follow the upper fifth Science throughout every day of the week.

FRANK. (*Indicating timetable.*) I must say, I think this is a really wonderful job.

ANDREW. Thank you. It has the merit of clarity, I think.

FRANK. I don't know what they'll do without you.

ANDREW. (*Without expression.*) They'll find somebody else, I expect.

Pause.

FRANK. What sort of job is this you're going to?

ANDREW. (*Looking at his wife for the first time.*) Hasn't Millie told you?

FRANK. She said it was a cr – a private school.

ANDREW. A crammer's – for backward boys. It is run by an old Oxford contemporary of mine who lives in Dorset. The work will not be so arduous as here and my doctor seems to think I will be able to undertake it without – er – danger –

FRANK. (*With genuine sympathy.*) It's the most rotten bad luck for you. I'm awfully sorry.

ANDREW. (*Raising his voice a little.*) My dear Hunter, there is nothing whatever to be sorry for. I am looking forward to the change –

There is a knock at the door.

ANDREW. Come in.

> TAPLOW *appears, a trifle breathless and guilty-looking. He carries a medicine bottle wrapped and sealed.*

Ah, Taplow. Good. You have been running, I see.

TAPLOW. Yes, sir. (*He hands the bottle to* MILLIE.)

ANDREW. There was a queue at the chemist's, I suppose?

TAPLOW. Yes, sir.

ANDREW. And doubtless an even longer one at Stewarts?

TAPLOW. Yes, sir – I mean – no, sir – I mean – (*He looks at* MILLIE.) – yes, sir.

MILLIE. You were late, yourself, Andrew.

ANDREW. Exactly. And for that I apologize, Taplow.

TAPLOW. That's all right, sir.

ANDREW. Luckily we have still a good hour before lock-up, so nothing has been lost –

FRANK. (*To* MILLIE.) May I use the short cut? I'm going back to my digs.

MILLIE. Yes. Go ahead. Come back soon. If Andrew hasn't finished we can sit in the garden. (*Moving to door.*) I'd better go and see about dinner.

> *She goes out at back.*

ANDREW. (*To* FRANK.) Taplow is desirous of obtaining a remove from my form, Hunter, so that he can spend the rest of his career here playing happily with the crucibles, retorts, and bunsen burners of your Science fifth.

FRANK. (*At door.*) Oh. Has he?

ANDREW. Has he what?

FRANK. Obtained his remove?

ANDREW. (*After a pause.*) He has obtained exactly what he deserves. No less; and certainly no more.

> TAPLOW *utters an explosion of mirth.*

> FRANK *nods, thoughtfully, and goes out through the garden door.* ANDREW *has caught sight of* TAPLOW'S *contorted face, but passes no remark on it. He sits at the table and makes a sign for* TAPLOW *to sit beside him. He picks up a text of the* Agamemnon *and* TAPLOW *does the same.*

Line thirteen hundred and ninety-nine. Begin.

TAPLOW. Chorus. We – are surprised at –

ANDREW. (*Automatically.*) We marvel at.

TAPLOW. We marvel at – thy tongue – how bold thou art – that
you –

ANDREW. Thou. (ANDREW'S *interruptions are automatic. His
thoughts are evidently far distant.*)

TAPLOW. Thou – can –

ANDREW. Canst –

TAPLOW. Canst – boastfully speak –

ANDREW. Utter such a boastful speech –

TAPLOW. Utter such a boastful speech – over – (*In a sudden rush
of inspiration.*) – the bloody corpse of the husband you have
slain –

   ANDREW *looks down at his text for the first time.* TAPLOW
   looks apprehensive

ANDREW. Taplow – I presume you are using a different text from
mine –

TAPLOW. No, sir.

ANDREW. That is strange for the line as I have it reads: $\eta \tau \iota \zeta$
$\tau o \iota \acute{o} \upsilon \delta \, \varepsilon' \pi' \, \acute{a} \upsilon \delta \rho \iota \, \kappa o \mu \pi \acute{a} \zeta \varepsilon \iota \varsigma \, \lambda \acute{o} \gamma o \upsilon$. However diligently I search
I can discover no 'bloody' – no 'corpse' – no 'you have slain'.
Simply 'husband' –

TAPLOW. Yes, sir. That's right.

ANDREW. Then why do you invent words that simply are not there?

TAPLOW. I thought they sounded better, sir. More exciting. After
all she did kill her husband, sir. (*With relish.*) She's just been revealed with his dead body and Cassandra's weltering in gore –

ANDREW. I am delighted at this evidence, Taplow, of your interest
in the rather more lurid aspects of dramaturgy, but I feel I must
remind you that you are supposed to be construing Greek, not
collaborating with Aeschylus.

TAPLOW. (*Greatly daring.*) Yes, but still, sir, translator's licence,
sir – I didn't get anything wrong – and after all it *is a* play and
not just a bit of Greek construe.

ANDREW. (*Momentarily at a loss.*) I seem to detect a note of end
of term in your remarks. I am not denying that the *Agamemnon*
is a play. It is perhaps the greatest play ever written –

TAPLOW. (*Quickly.*) I wonder how many people in the form think that?

Pause. TAPLOW *is instantly frightened of what he has said.*

Sorry, sir. Shall I go on?

ANDREW *does not answer. He sits motionless staring at his book.*

Shall I go on, sir?

There is another pause. ANDREW *raises his head slowly from his book.*

ANDREW. (*Murmuring gently, not looking at* TAPLOW.) When I was a very young man, only two years older than you are now, Taplow, I wrote, for my own pleasure, a translation of the *Agamemnon* – a very free translation – I remember – in rhyming couplets.

TAPLOW. The whole *Agamemnon* – in verse? That must have been hard work, sir.

ANDREW. It was hard work; but I derived great joy from it. The play had so excited and moved me that I wished to communicate, however imperfectly, some of that emotion to others. When I had finished it, I remember, I thought it very beautiful – almost more beautiful than the original.

TAPLOW. Was it ever published, sir?

ANDREW. No. Yesterday I looked for the manuscript while I was packing my papers. I was unable to find it. I fear it is lost – like so many other things. Lost for good.

TAPLOW. Hard luck, sir.

ANDREW *is silent again.* TAPLOW *steals a timid glance at him.*

Shall I go on, sir?

ANDREW, *with a slight effort, lowers his eyes again to his text.*

ANDREW. (*Raising his voice slightly.*) No. Go back and get that last line right.

TAPLOW, *out of* ANDREW'S *vision, as he thinks, makes a disgusted grimace in his direction.*

TAPLOW. That – thou canst utter such a boastful speech over thy husband –

ANDREW. Yes. And, now, if you would be so kind, you will do the line again, without the facial contortion which you just found necessary to accompany it –

TAPLOW *is just beginning the line again, when* MILLIE *appears hurriedly. She has on an apron.*

MILLIE. The headmaster's just coming up the drive. Don't tell him I'm in. The fish pie isn't in the oven yet.

She disappears.

TAPLOW, *who has jumped up on* MILLIE'S *entrance, turns hopefully to* ANDREW.

TAPLOW. I'd better go, hadn't I, sir? I mean – I don't want to be in the way –

ANDREW. We do not yet know that it is I the headmaster wishes to see. Other people live in this building.

There is a knock at the door.

ANDREW. Come in.

DR. FROBISHER *comes in. He looks more like a distinguished diplomat than a doctor of literature and classical scholar. He is in the middle fifties and goes to a very good tailor.*

FROBISHER. Ah, Crocker-Harris, I've caught you in. I'm so glad. I hope I'm not disturbing you?

ANDREW. I have been taking a pupil in extra work –

FROBISHER. On the penultimate day of term? That argues either great conscientiousness on your part or considerable backwardness on his.

ANDREW. Perhaps a combination of both –

FROBISHER. Quite so, but as this is my only chance of speaking to you before tomorrow, I think that perhaps your pupil will be good enough to excuse us – (*He turns politely to* TAPLOW.)

TAPLOW. Oh, yes, sir. That's really quite all right. (*He collects his books and dashes to the door.*)

ANDREW. I'm extremely sorry, Taplow. You will please explain to your father exactly what occurred over this lost hour and tell him that I shall in due course be writing to him to return the money involved –

TAPLOW. (*Hurriedly.*) Yes, sir. But please don't bother, sir. I know it's all right, sir. Thank you, sir.

He darts out.

FROBISHER. Have the Gilberts called on you, yet?

ANDREW. The Gilberts, sir? Who are they?

FROBISHER. Gilbert is your successor with the lower fifth. He is down here today with his wife, and as they will be taking over this flat I thought perhaps you wouldn't mind if they came in to look it over.

ANDREW. Of course not.

FROBISHER. I've told you about him, I think. He is a very brilliant young man and won exceptionally high honours at Oxford.

ANDREW. So I understand, sir.

FROBISHER. Not, of course, as high as the honours you yourself won there. He didn't, for instance, win the Chancellor's prize for Latin verse or the Gaisford.

ANDREW. He won the Hertford Latin, then?

FROBISHER. No. (*Mildly surprised.*) Did you win that, too?

ANDREW *nods*.

It's sometimes rather hard to remember that you are perhaps the most brilliant classical scholar we have ever had at the school –

ANDREW. You are very kind.

FROBISHER. (*Urbanely corrects his gaffe.*) Hard to remember, I mean – because of your other activities – your brilliant work on the school timetable, for instance, and also for your heroic battle for so long and against such odds with the soul-destroying lower fifth.

ANDREW. I have not found that my soul has been destroyed by the lower fifth, headmaster.

FROBISHER. I was joking, of course.

ANDREW. Oh. I see.

FROBISHER. Is your wife in?

ANDREW. Er – no. Not at the moment.

FROBISHER. I shall have a chance of saying goodbye to her to-morrow. I am rather glad I have got you to myself. I have a delicate matter – two rather delicate matters – to broach.

ANDREW. Please sit down.

FROBISHER. Thank you. (*He sits.*) Now you have been with us, in all, eighteen years, haven't you?

ANDREW *nods*.

It is extremely unlucky that you should have had to retire at so comparatively early an age and so short a time before you would have been eligible for a pension.

The HEADMASTER *is regarding his nails, as he speaks, studiously avoiding* ANDREW'S *gaze.*

ANDREW. Pension? (*After a pause.*) You have decided then, not to award me a pension?

FROBISHER. Not I, my dear fellow. It has nothing at all to do with me. It's the governors who, I'm afraid, have been forced to turn down your application. I put your case to them as well as I could, but they decided, with great regret, that they couldn't make an exception to the rule.

ANDREW. But I thought – my wife thought, that an exception was made some five years ago –

FROBISHER. Ah. In the case of Buller, you mean? True. But the circumstances with Buller were quite remarkable. It was, after all, in playing rugger against the school that he received that injury –

ANDREW. Yes. I remember.

FROBISHER. And then the governors received a petition from boys, old boys, and parents with over five hundred signatures.

ANDREW. I would have signed that petition myself, but through some oversight I was not asked –

FROBISHER. He was a splendid fellow, Buller. Splendid. Doing very well, too, now, I gather.

ANDREW. I'm delighted to hear it.

FROBISHER. Your own case, of course, is equally deserving. If not more so – for Buller was a younger man. Unfortunately – rules are rules – and are not made to be broken every few years; at any rate that is the governors' view.

ANDREW. I quite understand.

FROBISHER. I knew you would. Now might I ask you a rather impertinent question.

ANDREW. Certainly.

FROBISHER. You have, I take it, private means?

ANDREW. My wife has some.

FROBISHER. Ah, yes. Your wife has often told me of her family connections. I understand her father has a business in – Bradford – isn't it?

ANDREW. Yes. He runs a men's clothing shop in the Arcade.

FROBISHER. Indeed? Your wife's remarks had led me to imagine something a little more – extensive.

ANDREW. My father-in-law made a settlement on my wife at the time of our marriage. She has about three hundred a year of her own. I have nothing. Is that the answer to your question, headmaster?

FROBISHER. Yes. Thank you for your frankness. Now, this private school you are going to –

ANDREW. My salary at the crammer's is to be two hundred pounds a year.

FROBISHER. Quite so. With board and lodging, of course?

ANDREW. For eight months of the year.

FROBISHER. Yes, I see. (*He ponders a second.*) Of course, you know, there is the School Benevolent Fund that deals with cases of actual hardship –

ANDREW. There will be no actual hardship, headmaster.

FROBISHER. No. I am glad you take that view. I must admit, though, I had hoped that your own means had proved a little more ample. Your wife had certainly led me to suppose –

ANDREW. I am not denying that a pension would have been very welcome, headmaster, but I see no reason to quarrel with the governors' decision. What is the other delicate matter you have to discuss?

FROBISHER. Well, it concerns the arrangements at prize-giving tomorrow. You are, of course, prepared to say a few words.

ANDREW. I had assumed you would call on me to do so.

FROBISHER. Of course. It is always done, and I know the boys appreciate the custom.

ANDREW. I have already made a few notes of what I am going to say. Perhaps you would care –

FROBISHER. No, no. That isn't necessary at all. I know I can trust your discretion – not to say your wit. It will be, I know, a very moving moment for you – indeed for us all – but, as I'm sure you realize, it is far better to keep these occasions from becoming too heavy and distressing. You know how little the boys appreciate sentiment –

ANDREW. I do.

FROBISHER. That is why I've planned my own reference to you at the end of my speech to be rather more light and jocular than I would otherwise have made it.

ANDREW. I quite understand. I too have prepared a few little jokes and puns for my speech. One – a play of words on *vale,* farewell, and Wally, the Christian name of a backward boy in my class, is, I think, rather happy.

FROBISHER. Yes. (*He laughs belatedly.*) Very neat. That should go down extremely well.

ANDREW. I'm glad you like it.

FROBISHER. Well, now – there is a particular favour I have to ask of you in connection with the ceremony, and I know I shall not have to ask in vain. Fletcher, as you know, is leaving, too.

ANDREW. Yes. He is going into the City, they tell me.

FROBISHER. Yes. Now he is, of course, considerably junior to you. He has only been here – let me see – five years. But, as you know, he has done great things for our cricket – positive wonders, when you remember what doldrums we were in before he came –

ANDREW. Our win at Lord's this year was certainly most inspiriting –

FROBISHER. Exactly. Now I'm sure that tomorrow the boys will make the occasion of his farewell speech a tremendous demonstration of gratitude. The applause might go on for minutes – you know what the boys feel about Lord's – and I seriously doubt my ability to cut it short or even, I admit, the propriety of trying to do so. Now, you see the quandary in which I am placed?

ANDREW. Perfectly. You wish to refer to me and for me to make my speech before you come to Fletcher?

FROBISHER. It's extremely awkward, and I feel wretched about asking it of you – but it's more for your own sake than for mine or Fletcher's that I do. After all, a climax is what one must try to work up to on these occasions.

ANDREW. Naturally, headmaster, I wouldn't wish to provide an anti-climax.

FROBISHER. You really mustn't take it amiss, my dear fellow. The boys, in applauding Fletcher for several minutes and yourself say – for – well, for not quite so long – won't be making any personal demonstration between you. It will be quite impersonal – I assure you, quite impersonal.

ANDREW. I understand.

FROBISHER. (*Warmly.*) I knew you would, and I can hardly tell you how wisely I think you have chosen. Well now – as that is all my business, I think perhaps I had better be getting along. This has been a terribly busy day for me – for you too, I imagine.

ANDREW. Yes.

MILLIE *comes in. She has taken off her apron, and tidied herself up.*

MILLIE. (*In her social manner.*) Ah, headmaster. How good of you to drop in.

FROBISHER. (*More at home with her than with* ANDREW.) Mrs. Crocker-Harris. How are you?

They shake hands.

You're looking extremely well, I must say. Has anyone ever told you, Crocker-Harris, that you have a very attractive wife?

ANDREW. Many people, sir. But then I hardly need to be told.

MILLIE. Can I persuade you to stay a few moments and have a drink, headmaster. It's so rarely we have the pleasure of seeing you –

FROBISHER. Unfortunately, dear lady, I was just on the point of leaving. I have two frantic parents waiting for me at home. You are dining with us tomorrow – both of you, aren't you?

MILLIE. Yes, indeed – and so looking forward to it.

FROBISHER. I'm so glad. We can say our sad farewells then. (*To* ANDREW.) Au revoir, Crocker-Harris, and thank you very much.

ANDREW *bows.*

MILLIE *holds the door open for* FROBISHER *and follows him out into the hall.*

MILLIE. (*To* ANDREW *as she goes out with* FROBISHER.) Don't forget to take your medicine, dear, will you?

ANDREW. No.

FROBISHER. (*In the hall.*) Lucky invalid! To have such a very charming nurse –

MILLIE. (*Also in the hall.*) I really don't know what to say to all these compliments, headmaster. I don't believe you mean a word of them.

FROBISHER. Every word. Till tomorrow, then? Goodbye.

We hear the door slam. ANDREW *is staring out of the window.* MILLIE *reappears.*

MILLIE. Well? Do we get it?

ANDREW. (*Absently.*) Get what?

MILLIE. The pension, of course. Do we get it?

ANDREW. No.

MILLIE. My God! Why not?

ANDREW. It's against the rules.

MILLIE. Buller got it, didn't he? Buller got it? What's the idea of giving it to him and not to us?

ANDREW. The governors are afraid of establishing a precedent.

MILLIE. The mean old brutes! My God, what I wouldn't like to say to them! (*Rounding on* ANDREW.) And what did you say? Just sat there and made a joke in Latin, I suppose?

ANDREW. There wasn't very much I could say, in Latin or any other language.

MILLIE. Oh, wasn't there? I'd have said it all right. I wouldn't just have sat there twiddling my thumbs and taking it from that old phoney of a headmaster. But then, of course, I'm not a man.

ANDREW *is turning the pages of the* Agamemnon, *not looking at her.*

What do they expect you to do? Live on my money, I suppose.

ANDREW. There has never been any question of that. I shall be perfectly able to support myself.

MILLIE. Yourself? Doesn't the marriage service say something about the husband supporting his wife? Doesn't it? You ought to know?

ANDREW. Yes, it does.

MILLIE. And how do you think you're going to do that on two hundred a year?

ANDREW. I shall do my utmost to save some of it. You're welcome to it, if I can.

MILLIE. Thank you for precisely nothing.

ANDREW *underlines a word in the text he is reading.*

What else did the old fool have to say?

ANDREW. The headmaster? He wants me to make my speech tomorrow before instead of after Fletcher.

MILLIE. Yes. I knew he was going to ask that.

ANDREW. (*Without surprise.*) You knew?

MILLIE. Yes. He asked my advice about it a week ago. I told him to go ahead. I knew you wouldn't mind, and as there isn't a Mrs. Fletcher to make *me* look a fool, I didn't give two hoots.

There is a knock on the door.

Come in.

MR. *and* MRS. GILBERT *come in. He is about twenty-two, and his wife a year or so younger.*

GILBERT. Mr. Crocker-Harris?

ANDREW. (*Rising.*) Yes. Is it Mr. and Mrs. Gilbert? The headmaster told me you might look in.

MRS. GILBERT. I do hope we're not disturbing you.

ANDREW. Not at all. This is my wife.

MRS. GILBERT. How do you do.

ANDREW. Mr. and Mrs. Gilbert are our successors to this flat my dear.

MILLIE. Oh, yes. How nice to meet you both.

GILBERT. How do you do? We really won't keep you more than a second – my wife thought as we were here you wouldn't mind us taking a squint at our future home.

MRS. GILBERT. (*Unnecessarily.*) This is the drawing-room, I suppose?

MILLIE. That's right. Well, it's really a living-room. Andrew uses it as a study.

MRS. GILBERT. How charmingly you've done it!

MILLIE. Oh, do you think so? I'm afraid it isn't nearly as nice as I'd like to make it – but a schoolmaster's wife has to think of so many other things besides curtains and covers. Boys with dirty boots and a husband with leaky fountain pens, for instance.

MRS. GILBERT. Yes, I suppose so. Of course I haven't been a schoolmaster's wife for very long, you know.

GILBERT. Don't swank, darling. You haven't been a schoolmaster's wife at all yet.

MRS. GILBERT. Oh yes, I have – for two months. You were a schoolmaster when I married you.

GILBERT. Prep school doesn't count.

MILLIE. Have you only been married two months?

MRS. GILBERT. Two months and sixteen days.

GILBERT. Seventeen.

MILLIE. (*Sentimentally.*) Andrew, did you hear? They've only been married two months.

ANDREW. Indeed? Is that all?

MRS. GILBERT. (*At the garden door.*) Oh, look, darling. They've got a garden. It is yours, isn't it?

MILLIE. Oh, yes. It's only a pocket handkerchief, I'm afraid, but it's very useful to Andrew. He often works out there, don't you, dear?

ANDREW. Yes, indeed. I find it very agreeable.

MILLIE. Shall I show you the rest of the flat? It's a bit untidy, I'm afraid, but you must forgive that.

MRS. GILBERT. Oh, of course.

MILLIE. (*As they move to the door.*) And the kitchen is in a terrible mess. I'm in the middle of cooking dinner –

MRS. GILBERT. (*Breathlessly.*) Oh. Do you cook?

MILLIE. Oh, yes. I have to. We haven't had a maid for five years.

MRS. GILBERT. Oh, I do think that's wonderful of you, I'm scared stiff of having to do it for Peter – I know the first dinner I have to cook for him will wreck our married life –

GILBERT. Highly probable.

MILLIE. (*Following* MRS. GILBERT *out.*) Well, these days we've all got to try and do things we weren't really brought up to do.

They disappear.

ANDREW. (*To* GILBERT.) Don't you want to see the rest of the flat?

GILBERT. No. I leave all that sort of thing to my wife. She's the boss. I thought perhaps you could tell me something about the lower fifth.

ANDREW. What would you like to know?

GILBERT. Well, sir, quite frankly, I'm petrified.

ANDREW. I don't think you need to be. May I give you some sherry?

GILBERT. Thank you.

ANDREW. They are mostly boys of about fifteen or sixteen. They are not very difficult to handle.

GILBERT. The headmaster said you ruled them with a rod of iron. He called you the Himmler of the lower fifth.

ANDREW. Did he? The Himmler of the lower fifth? I think he exaggerated. I hope he exaggerated. The Himmler of the lower fifth?

GILBERT. (*Puzzled*.) He only meant that you kept the most wonderful discipline. I must say I do admire you for that. I couldn't even manage that with eleven-year-olds, so what I'll be like with fifteens and sixteens I shudder to think.

ANDREW. It is not so difficult. They aren't bad boys. Sometimes – a little wild and unfeeling, perhaps – but not bad. The Himmler of the lower fifth? Dear me!

GILBERT. Perhaps I shouldn't have said that. I've been tactless, I'm afraid.

ANDREW. Oh, no, please sit down.

GILBERT. Thank you, sir.

ANDREW. From the very beginning I realized that I didn't possess the knack of making myself liked – a knack that you will find you do possess.

GILBERT. Do you think so?

ANDREW. Oh, yes. I am quite sure of it. It is not a quality of great importance to a schoolmaster, though, for too much of it, as you may also find, is as great a danger as the total lack of it. Forgive me lecturing, won't you?

GILBERT. I want to learn.

ANDREW. I can only teach you from my own experience. For two or three years I tried very hard to communicate to the boys some of my own joy in the great literature of the past. Of course, I failed, as you will fail, nine hundred and ninety nine times out of a thousand. But a single success can atone and more than atone for all the failures in the world. And sometimes – very rarely, it is true – but sometimes I had that success. That was in the early years.

GILBERT. (*Eagerly listening*.) Please go on, sir.

ANDREW. In early years, too, I discovered an easy substitute for popularity. I had, of course, acquired – we all do – many little mannerisms and tricks of speech, and I found that the boys were beginning to laugh at me. I was very happy at that, and encouraged the boys' laughter by playing up to it. It made our relationship so very much easier. They didn't like me as a man, but they found me funny as a character, and you can teach more things by laughter than by earnestness – for I never did have much sense of humour. So, for a time, you see, I was quite a success as a schoolmaster – *(He stops.)* – I fear this is all very personal and embarrassing to you. Forgive me. You need have no fears about the lower fifth.

GILBERT. *(After a pause.)* I'm afraid I said something that hurt you very much. It's myself you must forgive, sir. Believe me, I'm desperately sorry.

ANDREW. There's no need. You were merely telling me what I should have known for myself. Perhaps I did in my heart, and hadn't the courage to acknowledge it. I knew, of course, that I was not only not liked, but now positively disliked. I had realized, too, that the boys – for many long years now – had ceased to laugh at me. I don't know why they no longer found me a joke. Perhaps it was my illness. No, I don't think it was that. Something deeper than that. Not a sickness of the body, but a sickness of the soul. At all events it didn't take much discernment on my part to realize I had become an utter failure as a schoolmaster. Still, stupidly enough, I hadn't realized that I was also feared. The Himmler of the lower fifth! I suppose that will become my epitaph.

GILBERT *is now deeply embarrassed and rather upset, but he remains silent.*

(With a mild laugh.) I cannot for the life of me imagine why I should choose to unburden myself to you – a total stranger – when I have been silent to others for so long. Perhaps it is because my very unworthy mantle is about to fall on your shoulders. If that is so I shall take a prophet's privilege and foretell that you will have a very great success with the lower fifth.

GILBERT. Thank you, sir. I shall do my best.

ANDREW. I can't offer you a cigarette, I'm afraid. I don't smoke.

GILBERT. That's all right, sir. Nor do I.

MILLIE *and* MRS. GILBERT *can be heard in the hall outside.*

MRS. GILBERT. *(Off.)* Thank you so much for showing me round.

MILLIE *and* MRS. GILBERT *come in.*

ANDREW. I trust your wife has found no major snags in your new flat.

MRS. GILBERT. No. None at all. Just imagine, Peter. Mr. and Mrs. Crocker-Harris first met each other on a holiday in the Lake District. Isn't that a coincidence!

GILBERT. (*A little distrait*.) Yes. Yes, it certainly is. On a walking tour, too?

MILLIE. Andrew was on a walking tour. No walking for me. I can't abide it. I was staying with my uncle – that's Sir William Bartop, you know – you may have heard of him?

GILBERT *and* MRS. GILBERT *try to look as though they had heard of him constantly.*

He'd taken a house near Windermere – quite a mansion it was really – rather silly for an old gentleman living alone – and Andrew knocked on our front-door one day and asked the footman for a glass of water. So my uncle invited him in to tea.

MRS. GILBERT. Our meeting wasn't quite as romantic as that.

GILBERT. I knocked her flat on her face.

MRS. GILBERT. Not with love at first sight. With the swing doors of our hotel bar. So, of course, then he apologized and –

GILBERT. (*Brusquely*.) Darling. The Crocker-Harrises, I'm sure, have far more important things to do than to listen to your detailed but inaccurate account of our very sordid little encounter. Why not just say I married you for your money and leave it at that? Come on, we must go.

MRS. GILBERT. (*To* MILLIE.) Isn't he awful to me?

MILLIE. Men have no souls, my dear. My husband is just as bad.

MRS. GILBERT. Goodbye, Mr. Crocker-Harris.

ANDREW. (*Bowing*.) Goodbye.

MRS. GILBERT. (*As she goes out with* MILLIE.) I think your idea about the dining-room is awfully good – if only 1 can get the permit –

MILLIE *and* MRS. GILBERT *go out.* GILBERT *has dallied to say goodbye alone to* ANDREW.

GILBERT. Goodbye, sir.

ANDREW. Er – you will, I know, respect the confidences I have just made to you –

GILBERT. I should hate you to think I wouldn't.

ANDREW. I am sorry to have embarrassed you. I don't know what came over me. I have not been very well, you know. Goodbye, my dear fellow, and my best wishes.

GILBERT. Thank you. The very best of good luck to you too, sir, in your future career.

ANDREW. My future career? Yes. Thank you.

GILBERT. Well, goodbye, sir.

GILBERT *goes out. We hear voices in the hall, cut short as the front-door closes.* MILLIE *comes back.*

MILLIE. Good-looking couple.

ANDREW. Very.

MILLIE. He looks as if he'd got what it takes. I should think he'll be a success all right.

ANDREW. That's what I thought.

MILLIE. I don't think it's much of a career, though – a schoolmaster – for a likely young chap like that.

ANDREW. I know you don't.

MILLIE. Still I bet when he leaves this place it won't be without a pension. It'll be roses, roses all the way, and tears and cheers and goodbye, Mr. Chips.

ANDREW. I expect so.

MILLIE. What's the matter with you?

ANDREW. Nothing.

MILLIE. You're not going to have another of your attacks, are you? You look dreadful.

ANDREW. I'm perfectly all right.

MILLIE. (*Indifferently.*) You know best. Your medicine's there, anyway, if you want it.

She goes out.

ANDREW, *left alone, continues for a time staring at the text he has been pretending to read. Then he puts one hand over his eyes. There is a knock on the door.*

ANDREW. Come in.

TAPLOW *appears timidly from behind the screen.*

(*Sharply.*) Yes, Taplow? What is it?

TAPLOW. Nothing, sir.

ANDREW. What do you mean, nothing?

TAPLOW. (*Timidly.*) I just came back to say goodbye, sir.

ANDREW. Oh. (*He gets up.*)

TAPLOW. I didn't have a chance with the head here. I rather dashed out, I'm afraid. I thought I'd just come back and – and wish you luck, sir.

ANDREW. Thank you, Taplow. That's good of you.

TAPLOW. I – er – thought this might interest you, sir. (*He quickly thrusts a small book into* ANDREW'S *hand.*)

ANDREW. What is it?

TAPLOW. Verse translation of the *Agamemnon,* sir. The Browning version. It's not much good. I've been reading it in the Chapel gardens.

ANDREW *very deliberately turns over the pages of the book.*

ANDREW. Very interesting, Taplow. (*He seems to have a little difficulty in speaking. He clears his throat and then goes on in his level, gentle voice.*) I know the translation, of course. It has its faults, I agree, but I think you will enjoy it more when you get used to the metre he employs.

He hands it to TAPLOW *who brusquely thrusts it back to him.*

TAPLOW. It's for you, sir.

ANDREW. For me?

TAPLOW. Yes, sir. I've written in it.

ANDREW *opens the fly-leaf and reads whatever is written there.*

ANDREW. Did you buy this?

TAPLOW. Yes, sir. It was only second-hand.

ANDREW. You shouldn't have spent your pocket-money this way.

TAPLOW. That's all right, sir. It wasn't very much. The price isn't still inside, is it?

ANDREW *carefully wipes his glasses and puts them on again.*

ANDREW. (*At length.*) No. Just what you've written. Nothing else.

TAPLOW. Good. I'm sorry you've got it already. I thought you probably would have –

ANDREW. I haven't got it already. I may have had it once. I can't remember. But I haven't got it now.

TAPLOW. That's all right, then.

ANDREW *continues to stare at* TAPLOW'S *inscription on the fly-leaf.*

(*Suspiciously.*) What's the matter, sir? Have I got the accent wrong on εὔμευϖς?

ANDREW. No. The perispomenon is perfectly correct.

He lowers the book and we notice his hands are shaking from some intense inner effort as he takes off his spectacles.

Taplow, would you be good enough to take that bottle of medicine, which you so kindly brought in, and pour me out one dose in a glass which you will find in the bathroom?

TAPLOW. (*Seeing something is wrong.*) Yes, sir.

ANDREW *sits at his seat by the table.*

ANDREW. The doses are clearly marked on the bottle. I usually put a little water with it.

TAPLOW. Yes, sir.

He takes the bottle and darts out.

ANDREW, *the moment he is gone, breaks down and begins to sob uncontrollably. He makes a desperate attempt, after a moment, to control himself, but when* TAPLOW *comes back his emotion is still very apparent.*

ANDREW. (*Taking the glass.*) Thank you. (*He drinks it, turning his back on* TAPLOW *as he does so. At length.*) You must forgive this exhibition of weakness, Taplow. The truth is I have been going through rather a strain lately.

TAPLOW. Of course, sir. I quite understand.

There is a knock on the garden door.

ANDREW. Come in.

FRANK *comes in.*

FRANK. Oh, sorry. I thought you'd be finished by now –

ANDREW. Come in, Hunter, do. It's perfectly all right. Our lesson was over some time ago, but Taplow most kindly came back to say goodbye.

FRANK, *taking in* TAPLOW'S *rather startled face and* ANDREW'S *obvious emotion, looks a little puzzled.*

FRANK. Are you sure I'm not intruding?

ANDREW. No, no. I want you to see this book that Taplow has
given me, Hunter. Look. (*He hands it to* HUNTER.) A translation of the *Agamemnon* by Robert Browning. Do you see the
inscription he has put into it?

FRANK. Yes, but it's no use to me, I'm afraid. I never learnt Greek.

ANDREW. Then we'll have to translate it for him, won't we,
Taplow? (*Reciting by heart.*) τὸν κρατοῦντα μαλθακῶς θεὸς
πρόσωθεν εὐμενῶς προσδέρκεται. That means – in a rough
translation: 'God from afar looks graciously upon a gentle
master.' It comes from a speech of Agamemnon's to
Clytaemnestra.

FRANK. I see. Very pleasant and very apt. (*He hands the book
back to* ANDREW.)

ANDREW. Very pleasant. But perhaps not, after all, so very apt.

*He turns quickly away from both of them as emotion once more
seems about to overcome him.* FRANK *brusquely jerks his head
to the bewildered* TAPLOW *to get out.* TAPLOW *nods.*

TAPLOW. Goodbye, sir, and the best of luck.

ANDREW. Goodbye, Taplow, and thank you very much.

TAPLOW *flees quickly.* FRANK *watches* ANDREW'S *back
with a mixture of embarrassment and sympathy.*

(*Turning at length, slightly recovered.*) Dear me, what a fool I
made of myself in front of that boy. And in front of you, Hunter.
I can't imagine what you must think of me.

FRANK. Nonsense.

ANDREW. I am not a very emotional person, as you know, but
there was something so very touching and kindly about his
action, and coming as it did just after – (*He stops, then glances
at the book in his hand.*) This is a very delightful thing to have,
don't you think?

FRANK. Delightful.

ANDREW. The quotation, of course, he didn't find entirely by
himself. I happened to make some little joke about the line in
form the other day. But he must have remembered it all the
same to have found it so readily – and perhaps he means it.

FRANK. I'm sure he does, or he wouldn't have written it.

MILLIE *comes in.*

MILLIE. Hullo, Frank. I'm glad you're in time. (*She picks up the medicine bottle and the glass from the table and puts them aside. To* FRANK.) Lend me a cigarette. I've been gasping for one for an hour.

FRANK *once more extends his case and* MILLIE *takes a cigarette which he lights.*

FRANK. Your husband has just had a very nice present.

MILLIE. Oh? Who from?

FRANK. Taplow.

MILLIE. (*Smiling.*) Oh, Taplow. Let's see. (*She takes the book from* ANDREW.)

ANDREW. He bought it with his own pocket-money, Millie, and wrote a very charming inscription inside.

FRANK. God looks kindly upon a gracious master.

ANDREW. No – not gracious – gentle, I think – τòυ κρατοûντα μαλθακῶς – yes I think gentle is the better translation. I would rather have had this present than almost anything I can think of.

Pause. MILLIE *laughs suddenly.*

MILLIE. The artful little beast –

FRANK. (*Urgently.*) Millie –

ANDREW. Artful? Why artful?

MILLIE *looks at* FRANK *who is staring meaningly at her.*

Why artful, Millie?

MILLIE *laughs again, quite lightly, and turns from* FRANK *to* ANDREW.

MILLIE. My dear, because I came into this room this afternoon to find him giving an imitation of you to Frank here. Obviously he was scared stiff I was going to tell you, and you'd ditch his remove or something. I don't blame him for trying a few bobs' worth of appeasement.

She hands the book back to ANDREW *who stands quite still looking down at it.*

ANDREW. (*Nodding, at length.*) I see. (*He puts the book gently on the table and walks to the door.*)

MILLIE. Where are you going, dear? Dinner's nearly ready.

ANDREW. Only to my room for a moment. I won't be long.

He takes the medicine bottle and a glass.

MILLIE. You've just had a dose of that, dear. I shouldn't have another, if I were you.

ANDREW. I am allowed two at a time.

MILLIE. Well, see it is two and no more, won't you?

ANDREW *meets her eye for a moment, at the door, then goes out quietly.*

MILLIE *turns to* FRANK *with an expression half defiant and half ashamed.*

FRANK. (*With a note of real repulsion in his voice.*) Millie! My God! How could you?

MILLIE. Well, why not? Why should he be allowed his comforting little illusions? I'm not.

FRANK. (*Advancing on her.*) Listen. You're to go to his room now and tell him that was a lie.

MILLIE. Certainly not. It wasn't a lie.

FRANK. If you don't, I will.

MILLIE. I shouldn't, if I were you. It'll only make things worse. He won't believe you.

FRANK. (*Moving.*) We'll see about that.

MILLIE. Go ahead. See what happens. He knows I don't lie to him. He knows what I told him was the truth, and he won't like your sympathy. He'll think you're making fun of him, like Taplow.

FRANK *hesitates at the door then comes slowly back into the room.* MILLIE *watches him, a little frightened.*

FRANK. (*At length.*) We're finished, Millie – you and I.

MILLIE. (*Laughing.*) Frank, really! Don't be hysterical.

FRANK. I'm not. I mean it.

MILLIE. (*Lightly.*) Oh, yes, you mean it. Of course you mean it. Now just sit down, dear, and relax and forget all about artful little boys and their five-bob presents, and talk to me.

She touches his arm. He moves away from her brusquely.

FRANK. Forget? If I live to be a hundred I shall never forget that little glimpse you've just given me of yourself.

MILLIE. Frank – you're making a frightening mountain out of an absurd little molehill.

FRANK. Of course, but the mountain I'm making in my imagination is so frightening that I'd rather try to forget both it and the repulsive little molehill that gave it birth. But as I know I never can, I tell you, Millie – from this moment you and I are finished.

MILLIE. (*Quietly.*) You can't scare me, Frank. I know that's what you're trying to do, but you can't do it.

FRANK. (*Quietly.*) I'm not trying to scare you, Millie. I'm telling you the simple truth. I'm not coming to Bradford.

MILLIE. (*After a pause, with an attempt at bravado.*) All right, my dear, if that's the way you feel about it. Don't come to Bradford.

FRANK. Right. Now I think you ought to go to your room and look after Andrew. I'm leaving.

MILLIE *runs quickly to stop him.*

MILLIE. What is this? Frank, I don't understand, really I don't. What have I done?

FRANK. I think you know what you've done, Millie. Go and look after Andrew.

MILLIE. Andrew? Why this sudden concern for Andrew?

FRANK. Because I think he's just been about as badly hurt as a human being can be, and as he's a sick man and in a rather hysterical state it might be a good plan to go and see how he is.

MILLIE. (*Scornfully.*) Hurt? Andrew hurt? You can't hurt Andrew. He's dead.

FRANK. Why do you hate him so much, Millie?

MILLIE. Because he keeps me from you.

FRANK. That isn't true.

MILLIE. Because he's not a man at all.

FRANK. He's a human being.

MILLIE. You've got a fine right to be so noble about him, after deceiving him for six months.

FRANK. Twice in six months – at your urgent invitation.

MILLIE *slaps his face, in a violent paroxysm of rage.*

Thank you for that. I deserved it. I deserve a lot worse than that, too –

MILLIE. (*Running to him.*) Frank, forgive me – I didn't mean it –

FRANK. (*Quietly.*) You'd better have the truth, Millie. It had to come some time. I've never loved you. I've never told you I loved you.

MILLIE. I know, Frank, 1 know – I've always accepted that.

FRANK. You asked me just now if I was running away from you. Well, I was.

MILLIE. I knew that too.

FRANK. But I was coming to Bradford. It was going to be the very last time I was ever going to see you and at Bradford I would have told you that.

MILLIE. You wouldn't. You wouldn't. You've tried to tell me that so often before – and I've always stopped you somehow – somehow. I would have stopped you again.

FRANK. (*Quietly.*) I don't think so, Millie. Not this time.

MILLIE. Frank, I don't care what humiliations you heap on me. I know you don't give two hoots for me as a person. I've always known that. I've never minded so long as you cared for me as a woman. And you do, Frank. You do. You do, don't you?

FRANK *is silent.*

It'll be all right at Bradford, you see. It'll be all right, there –

FRANK. I'm not coming to Bradford, Millie.

The door opens slowly and ANDREW *comes in, carrying the bottle of medicine. He hands it to* MILLIE *and passes on.* MILLIE *quickly holds the bottle up to the light.* ANDREW *turns and sees her.*

ANDREW. (*Gently.*) You should know me well enough by now, my dear, to realize how unlikely it is that I should ever take an overdose.

MILLIE, *without a word, puts the bottle down and goes out.*

ANDREW *goes to a cupboard at back and produces a decanter of sherry and a glass.*

FRANK. I'm not staying to dinner, I'm afraid.

ANDREW. Indeed? I'm sorry to hear that. You'll have a glass of sherry?

FRANK. No, thank you.

ANDREW. You will forgive me if I do.

FRANK. Of course.

ANDREW *pours himself a glass.*

Perhaps I'll change my mind.

ANDREW *pours* FRANK *a glass.*

About Taplow –

ANDREW. Oh, yes?

FRANK. It *is* perfectly true that he was imitating you. I, of course, was mostly to blame in that, and I'm very sorry.

ANDREW. That is perfectly all right. Was it a good imitation?

FRANK. No.

ANDREW. I expect it was. Boys are often very clever mimics.

FRANK. We talked about you, of course, before that. He said – you probably won't believe this, but I thought I ought to tell you – he said he liked you very much.

ANDREW *smiles slightly.*

ANDREW. Indeed?

FRANK. I can remember very clearly his exact words. He said: 'He doesn't seem to like people to like him – but in spite of that, I do – very much.' (*Lightly.*) So you see it looks after all as if the book might not have been a mere question of – appeasement.

ANDREW. The book? (*He picks it up.*) Dear me! What a lot of fuss about a little book – and a not very good little book at that. (*He drops it on the table.*)

FRANK. I would like you to believe me.

ANDREW. Possibly you would, my dear Hunter; but I can assure you I am not particularly concerned about Taplow's views of my character: or about yours either, if it comes to that.

FRANK. (*Hopelessly.*) I think you should keep that book all the same. You may find it'll mean something to you after all.

ANDREW. Exactly. It will mean a perpetual reminder to myself of the story with which Taplow is at this very moment regaling his friends in the House. 'I gave the Crock a book, to buy him off, and he blubbed. The Crock blubbed. I tell you I was there. I saw it. The Crock blubbed.' My mimicry is not as good as his, I fear. Forgive me. And now let us leave this idiotic subject and talk of more pleasant things. Do you like this sherry? I got it on my last visit to London –

FRANK. If Taplow ever breathes a word of that story to any one at all, I'll murder him. But he won't. And if you think I will you greatly underestimate my character as well as his. (*He drains his glass.*) Goodbye.

ANDREW. Are you leaving so soon? Goodbye, my dear fellow.

He does not get up nor offer to shake hands. FRANK *goes to the window.*

FRANK. As this is the last time I shall probably ever see you I'm going to offer you a word of advice.

ANDREW. (*Politely.*) I shall be glad to listen to it.

FRANK. Leave your wife.

Pause. ANDREW *takes a sip of his sherry.*

ANDREW. (*At length.*) So that you may the more easily carry on your intrigue with her?

FRANK *stares at him, then comes back into the room.*

FRANK. How long have you known that?

ANDREW. Since it first began.

FRANK. How did you find out?

ANDREW. By information.

FRANK. By whose information?

ANDREW. By someone's whose word I could hardly discredit.

Pause.

FRANK. (*Slowly, with repulsion.*) No! That's too horrible to think of.

ANDREW. Nothing is ever too horrible to think of, Hunter. It is simply a question of facing facts.

FRANK. She might have told you a lie. Have you faced that fact?

ANDREW. She never tells me a lie. In twenty years she has never told me a lie. Only the truth.

FRANK. This was a lie.

ANDREW. No, my dear Hunter. Do you wish me to quote you dates?

FRANK. (*Still unable to believe it.*) And she told you six months ago?

ANDREW. Isn't it seven?

FRANK. (*Savagely.*) Then why have you allowed me inside your home? Why haven't you done something – reported me to the governors – anything – made a scene, knocked me down?

ANDREW. Knocked you down?

FRANK. You didn't have to invite me to dinner.

ANDREW. My dear Hunter, if, over the last twenty years, I had allowed such petty considerations to influence my choice of dinner guests I would have found it increasingly hard to remember which master to invite and which to refuse. You see, Hunter, you mustn't flatter yourself you are the first. My information is a good deal better than yours, you understand. It's authentic.

Pause.

FRANK. She's evil.

ANDREW. That's hardly a kindly epithet to apply to a lady whom, I gather, you have asked to marry.

FRANK. Did she tell you that?

ANDREW. She's a dutiful wife. She tells me everything.

FRANK. That, at least, was a lie.

ANDREW. She never lies.

FRANK. That was a lie. Do you want the truth? Can you bear the truth?

ANDREW. I can bear anything.

FRANK. What I did, I did cold-bloodedly out of weakness and ignorance and crass stupidity. I'm bitterly, bitterly ashamed of myself, but, in a sense, I'm glad you know, though I'd rather a thousand times that you'd heard it from me than from your wife. I won't ask you to forgive me. I can only tell you, with complete truth, that the only emotion she has ever succeeded in arousing in me she aroused in me for the first time ten minutes ago – an intense and passionate disgust.

ANDREW. What a delightfully chivalrous statement –

FRANK. Forget chivalry, Crock, for God's sake. Forget all your fine Mosaic scruples. You must leave her – it's your only chance.

ANDREW. She's my wife, Hunter. You seem to forget that. As long as she wishes to remain my wife, she may.

FRANK. She's out to kill you.

ANDREW. My dear Hunter, if that was indeed her purpose, you should know by now that she fulfilled it long ago.

FRANK. Why won't you leave her?

ANDREW. Because I wouldn't wish to add another grave wrong to one I have already done her.

FRANK. What wrong have you done her?

ANDREW. To marry her.

Pause. FRANK *stares at him in silence.*

You see, my dear Hunter, she is really quite as much to be pitied as I. We are both of us interesting subjects for your microscope. Both of us needing from the other something that would make life supportable for us, and neither of us able to give it. Two kinds of love. Hers and mine. Worlds apart, as I know now, though when I married her I didn't think they were incompatible. In those days I hadn't thought that her kind of love – the love she requires and which I was unable to give her – was so important that its absence would drive out the other kind of love – the kind of love that I require and which I thought, in my folly, was by far the greater part of love. I may have been, you see, Hunter, a brilliant classical scholar, but I was woefully ignorant of the facts of life. I know better now, of course. I know that in both of us, the love that we should have borne each other has turned to bitter hatred. That's all the problem is. Not a very unusual one, I venture to think – nor nearly as tragic as you seem to imagine. Merely the problem of an unsatisfied wife and a henpecked husband. You'll find it all over the world. It is usually, I believe, a subject for farce. And now, if you have to leave us, my dear fellow, please don't let me detain you any longer.

He turns his back deliberately on FRANK, *who makes no move to go.*

FRANK. Don't go to Bradford. Stay here, until you take up your new job.

ANDREW. I think I've already told you I'm not interested in your advice.

FRANK. Leave her. It's the only way.

ANDREW. (*Violently.*) Will you please go!

FRANK. All right. I'd just like you to say goodbye to me, properly, though. Will you? I shan't see you again.

ANDREW *rises and walks slowly over to him.*

I know you don't want my pity, but I would like to be of some help.

ANDREW. If you think, by this expression of kindness, Hunter, that you can get me to repeat the shameful exhibition of emotion I made to Taplow a moment ago, I must tell you that you have no chance. My hysteria over that book just now was no more than a sort of reflex action of the spirit. The muscular twitchings of a corpse. It can never happen again.

FRANK. A corpse can be revived.

ANDREW. I don't believe in miracles.

FRANK. Don't you? Funnily enough, as a scientist, I do.

ANDREW. Your faith would be touching, if I were capable of being touched by it.

FRANK. You are, I think. (*After a pause.*) I'd like to come and visit you at this crammer's.

ANDREW. That is an absurd suggestion.

FRANK. I suppose it is rather, but all the same I'd like to do it. May I?

ANDREW. Of course not.

FRANK. Your term begins on the first of September, doesn't it?

ANDREW. I tell you the idea is quite childish –

FRANK. I could come about the second week.

ANDREW. You would be bored to death. So, probably, would I.

FRANK. (*Glancing at pocket calendar.*) Let's say Monday the twelfth, then.

ANDREW. (*His hands beginning to tremble again.*) Say anything you like, only please go. Please go, Hunter.

FRANK. (*Writing in his book and not looking at* ANDREW.) That's fixed, then. Monday, September the twelfth. Will you remember that?

ANDREW. (*After a pause, speaking with difficulty.*) I suppose I'm at least as likely to remember it as you are.

FRANK. That's fixed, then. (*He slips the book into his pocket and puts out his hand.*) Goodbye, until then.

ANDREW, *after hesitation, shakes his hand.*

ANDREW. Goodbye.

FRANK. May I go out through your garden?

ANDREW. (*Nodding.*) Of course.

FRANK. I'm off to have a quick word with Taplow. By the way, may I take him a message from you?

ANDREW. What message?

FRANK. Has he or has he not got his remove?

ANDREW. He has.

FRANK. May I tell him?

ANDREW. It is highly irregular. Yes, you may.

FRANK. Good. (*He turns to go then turns back.*) Oh, by the way, I'd better have the address of that crammer's. (*He takes out his notebook and points his pencil, ready to write.*)

MILLIE *comes in with tray, dishes, and cutlery. She starts to set the table.*

MILLIE. Dinner's ready. You're staying, Frank, aren't you?

FRANK. (*Politely.*) No. I'm afraid not. (*To* ANDREW.) What's that address?

ANDREW. (*After great hesitation.*) The Old Deanery, Malcombe, Dorset.

FRANK. I'll write to you and you can let me know about trains. (*To* MILLIE.) Goodbye. (*To* ANDREW.) Goodbye.

He goes out. MILLIE *is silent for a moment. Then she laughs.*

MILLIE. That's a laugh, I must say.

ANDREW. What's a laugh, my dear?

MILLIE. You inviting him to stay with you.

ANDREW. I didn't. He suggested it.

MILLIE. He's coming to Bradford.

ANDREW. Yes. I remember your telling me so.

MILLIE *comes close to* ANDREW.

MILLIE. He's coming to Bradford. He's not going to you.

ANDREW. The likeliest contingency is, that he's not going to either of us. Shall we have dinner?

MILLIE. He's coming to Bradford.

ANDREW. I expect so. Oh, by the way, I'm not. I shall be staying here until I go to Dorset.

MILLIE. (*Indifferently.*) Suit yourself – what makes you think I'll join you there?

ANDREW. I don't.

MILLIE. You needn't expect me.

ANDREW. I don't think either of us has the right to expect anything further from the other.

The telephone rings.

ANDREW. I don't. Excuse me. (*He picks up the receiver.*) Hullo . . . Yes, headmaster . . . The timetable? . . . It's perfectly simple. The middle fourth B division will take a ten-minute break on Tuesdays and a fifteen-minute break on alternate Wednesdays; while exactly the reverse procedure will apply to the lower Shell, C division. I thought I had sufficiently explained that on my chart . . . Oh, I see . . . Thank you, that is very good of you . . . yes. I think you will find it will work out quite satisfactorily . . . Oh, by the way, headmaster. I have changed my mind about the prize-giving ceremony. I intend to speak after, instead of before, Fletcher, as is my privilege . . . Yes, I quite understand, but I am now seeing the matter in a different light . . . I know, but I am of opinion that occasionally an anti-climax can be surprisingly effective. Goodbye. (*He rings off and goes and sits at table.*) Come along, my dear. We mustn't let our dinner get cold.

Curtain.

HARLEQUINADE

Foreword to Mr. Wilmot

You and I both know, dear Mr. Wilmot – who better? – that if the correct definition of farce is 'the theatrical presentation of unlikely events' then this play belies its label. I freely admit, dear Mr. Wilmot, that, in calling it a farce I am most grossly deceiving that great and innocent Public who know so much about Life and so little about the Theatre. For this misnomer, therefore, I beg, dear Mr. Wilmot, your gracious forgiveness. For you, I know, would more properly be inclined to call it tragedy; so, too, in all probability, the critics; and so too, perhaps, even that great and still innocent Public who know so much about the Theatre and so little about Life; while I, myself, would indeed agree with you all did not the claim of decorum, to which you, dear Mr. Wilmot, should ever lend as lively an ear as myself, demand that I continue to call this play what it palpably is not – to wit, a farce.

Characters

ARTHUR GOSPORT
EDNA SELBY
DAME MAUD GOSPORT
JACK WAKEFIELD
GEORGE CHUDLEIGH
FIRST HALBERDIER
SECOND HALBERDIER
MISS FISHLOCK
FRED INGRAM
JOHNNY
MURIEL PALMER
TOM PALMER
MR. BURTON
JOYCE LANGLAND
POLICEMAN

Scene: *the stage of a theatre in a Midlands town.*

Harlequinade was first produced in a double-bill with *The Browning Version*, under the joint title, *Playbill*, at the Phoenix Theatre, London, on September 8th, 1948, with the following cast:

ARTHUR GOSPORT	Eric Portman
EDNA SELBY	Mary Ellis
DAME MAUD GOSPORT	Marie Löhr
JACK WAKEFIELD	Hector Ross
GEORGE CHUDLEIGH	Kenneth Edwards
FIRST HALBERDIER	Peter Scott
SECOND HALBERDIER	Basil Howes
MISS FISHLOCK	Noel Dyson
FRED INGRAM	Anthony Oliver
JOHNNY	Henry Bryce
MURIEL PALMER	Thelma Ruby
TOM PALMER	Patrick Jordan
MR. BURTON	Campbell Cotts
JOYCE LANGLAND	Henryetta Edwards
POLICEMAN	Manville Tarrant

The play directed by PETER GLENVILLE

Harlequinade

Scene: the stage of a theatre in a Midlands town. The lights are out on the rise of the curtain. They come on gradually to reveal the graceful figure of ARTHUR GOSPORT *as he enters. He is dressed in doublet and tights*

ARTHUR. (*Shouting over his shoulder.*) He jests at scars that never felt a wound.

The lights now reveal enough for us to see that he has found himself in an unmistakable, if rather severely functional, fifteenth-century Italian garden, with, at one side, the balcony of a house, from the window of which is shining a light.

But, soft! What light through yonder window breaks?
It is the east, and Juliet is the sun!
Arise, fair sun, and kill the envious moon,
Who is already sick and pale with grief,
That thou her maid art far more fair than she:
Be not her maid, since she is envious;
Her vestal livery is but sick and green,
And none but fools do wear it; cast it off.

Juliet, in the person of EDNA SELBY, *appears at the balcony above.*

It is my lady; O, it is my love!
O, that she knew she were!

EDNA *emits a melodious sigh and gives a sad shake of the head.*

She speaks, yet she says nothing; and what of that?
Her eye discourses, I will answer it.

He comes forward, then leaps back.

I am too bold, 'tis not to me she speaks:
Two of the fairest stars in all the heaven,
Having some business, do entreat her eyes
To twinkle in their spheres till they return.
What if her eyes were there, they in her head?
The brightness of her cheek would shame those stars,
As daylight doth a lamp; her eyes in heaven
Would through the airy region stream so bright
That birds would sing, and think it were not night.

EDNA *emits another melodious sigh, and rests her cheek thoughtfully upon her hand.*

See how she leans her cheek upon her hand!
O, that I were a glove upon that hand,
That I might touch that cheek!

EDNA. Ah me!

ARTHUR .   She speaks:
O, speak again, bright angel! for thou art
As glorious to this night, being o'er my head,
As is a winged messenger of heaven
Unto the white-upturned wondering eyes
Of mortals that fall back to gaze on him
When he bestrides the lazy-pacing clouds
And sails upon the bosom of the air.

EDNA. O Romeo, Romeo! Wherefore art thou Romeo?
Deny thy father and refuse thy name;
Or, if thou wilt not, be but sworn my love,
And I'll no longer be a Capulet.

ARTHUR. (*Aside.*) Shall I hear more, or shall I speak at this?

In the intense excitement of his passion he gives a boyish leap on to a garden stool. EDNA'S *glance momentarily wavers from the upper regions of the theatre, on which her eyes have been sentimentally fixed since the beginning of the scene.*

EDNA. 'Tis but thy name that is my enemy;
Thou art thyself though, not a Montague.
What's Montague?

Darling, are you going to do that tonight?

ARTHUR. What?

EDNA. That little jump.

ARTHUR. Well – yes – I thought I would. Why? Does it bother you?

EDNA. No, darling. Just so long as I know, that's all.

ARTHUR. Sorry, darling. That's quite all right. Let's go back. (*To prompt corner.*) Yes?

JOHNNY, (*From prompt corner.*) 'Tis but thy name –

EDNA. (*Sharply.*) No. Before that. I want to give Mr. Gosport the cue for his little jump.

JOHNNY. (*Off.*) What little jump, Miss Selby?

EDNA. The little jump he does on to that stool.

Enter JOHNNY.

JOHNNY. Mr. Gosport doesn't do a little jump, Miss Selby.

EDNA. Yes, he does do a little jump. He's just done a little jump.

JOHNNY. He's never done a little jump before.

EDNA. I know he's never done a little jump before. But he's doing a little jump now. He's just put a little jump in.

ARTHUR. Look – I don't think I'll do the little jump, after all.

EDNA. Yes, you shall, my darling. You shall do the little jump. It looked very charming – very youthful. (*To prompt corner.*) When Mr. Gosport says: 'Shall I speak at this?' he does a little jump on to a stool. Now what's my line before that?

JOHNNY. (*Going off.*) And I'll no longer be a Capulet.

EDNA. (*Resuming her pose.*)
Or, if thou wilt not, be but sworn my love,
And I'll no longer be a Capulet.

ARTHUR *does his leap again, only this time it is, perhaps, not quite so boyish as before.*

ARTHUR. Shall I hear more or shall I speak at this?

EDNA. 'Tis but thy name that is my enemy;
Thou art thyself though, not a Montague.
What's Montague?

While speaking she has appeared to be struggling to keep her composure. She now loses the battle and laughs outright.

Sorry, darling.

ARTHUR. Does it look awfully silly? I won't do it, then.

EDNA. Oh no – you must do it. Come on. Let's try again.

ARTHUR. No. I won't do it if it's as funny as all that. I only thought it might help the boyishness of the line, that's all.

EDNA. And it does. It looks very boyish. (*To prompt corner.*) Doesn't it look boyish, Johnny?

JOHNNY. (*Off.*) Very boyish, Miss Selby.

EDNA, I was only laughing at your suddenly putting in a thing like that, after our having done this play so many hundreds of times together and never a little jump in fifteen years until now – just before a first night.

ARTHUR. All right. All right. Let's forget the whole thing. I'll say the line standing as still as the Rock of Ages, and looking just about twice as old – let's go on.

EDNA. It's silly to say that, Arthur. If you feel you're too old for the part you'll only get a complex about it.

ARTHUR. I am much too old for the part. I'm not seventeen.

EDNA. Well, if it comes to that, darling, I'm not thirteen, but I shan't let that worry me tonight. It's all up here – (She *taps her forehead*.) – it's not just a question of doing little jumps –

ARTHUR. I am not doing any little jump. That's dead, once and for all. Now, for God's sake, let's go on.

EDNA. Besides, it's silly to think you don't look young. That wig is very, very becoming. (*She shields her eyes and looks over the footlights at the audience*.) Auntie Maud! Are you in front, dear?

DAME MAUD GOSPORT *appears from the wings. She is an imposing old lady dressed as the Nurse.*

DAME MAUD. I've just come from in front, dear. What is it?

EDNA. How did you think Arthur looked?

DAME MAUD. Far too old.

EDNA. Oh. Too much light on him?

DAME MAUD. Far too much.

ARTHUR. What about Edna, Auntie Maud? How did she look?

DAME MAUD. Far too old, too.

ARTHUR. Too much light on her too?

DAME MAUD. Yes. Far too much.

EDNA. I don't think Auntie Maud sees very well. Do you, Auntie Maud, dear? (*To* ARTHUR, *in an undertone*.) She's getting so shortsighted, you know, Arthur –

DAME MAUD. (*Firmly*.) Yes, I do. I see very well. I had my specs on, and I was right at the back, and you both looked far too old.

She goes off.

ARTHUR. (*Calling*.) Jack! Jack! Where's the stage manager?

JACK WAKEFIELD, *the stage manager, comes on from the prompt corner. He is a grave-faced young man in the late twenties.*

JACK. Yes, Mr. Gosport?

ARTHUR. The lighting for this scene has gone mad. This isn't our plot. There's far too much light. What's gone wrong with it?

JACK. I think the trouble is they've crept in numbers two and three too early. (*Calling up to the flies.*) Will – check your plot, please. Number two and three spots should be down to a quarter instead of full.

VOICE. (*From above.*) O.K.

JACK. And you've got your floats too high, too, You're burning Mr. Gosport up –

EDNA. What about me? I've got an enormous searchlight on me from somewhere out there.

JACK. (*Looking.*) That's the front of house, Miss Selby. It's in the plot.

EDNA. Well, take it out –

ARTHUR. No, you can't. You've got to have some light on this scene. We can't have it played as just our two voices coming out of pitch darkness, much as we both might like to.

EDNA. Well, I don't see why you should skulk about in romantic moonlight while I'm on my balcony, being burnt to a cinder by Eddystone Lighthouse.

ARTHUR. Let me see that plot.

DAME MAUD *comes on to join* EDNA *on balcony.*

DAME MAUD. As you've stopped, dear, I thought you wouldn't mind if I gave you one or two teeny little hints about this scene. It's the first time I've seen it from the front. You don't mind an old lady's interference, do you, dear?

EDNA. (*Rather too sweetly.*) No, of course not, Auntie Maud. You know how delighted I always am to have your teeny hints.

JACK *and* ARTHUR *pay no attention to* DAME MAUD, *continuing to rearrange the lighting.*

JACK. Take it right down, Will . . . That's it.

DAME MAUD (*To* EDNA.) Now when I played Juliet I used to rest my hand on my cheek, like this – (*She demonstrates.*) using just the very tips of my fingers. Now as you do it you look just a little like Rodin's *Thinker.*

EDNA. Oh. Do I?

ARTHUR. (*Lighting.*) That's too low. Now bring it up a bit.

JACK. Bring it up, Will.

EDNA. Well, you know, Auntie Maud, dear, tastes have changed a little since you played Juliet with Arthur's father.

DAME MAUD. I know they have, dear, and more's the pity.

EDNA. The theatre's gone through a revolution since 1900.

DAME MAUD. It was 1914 I played Juliet, dear. I remember the date well, because the declaration of war damaged our business so terribly.

EDNA There's been another war since then, Auntie Maud, and I don't think you quite understand the immense change that has come over the theatre in the last few years. You see, dear – I know it's difficult for you to grasp, but the theatre of today has at last acquired a social conscience, and a social purpose. Why else do you think we're opening at this rathole of a theatre instead of the Opera House, Manchester?

DAME MAUD. Oh, I didn't know it was social purpose that brought us here. I thought it was C.E.M.A.

EDNA. C.E.M.A. is social purpose.

DAME MAUD. Is it, dear? Fancy!

ARTHUR. (*Still lighting*.) Take it down. That's too high.

JACK. (*Calling*.) Too high, Will.

An old actor, GEORGE CHUDLEIGH, *comes on to the stage. He is dressed as a fifteenth-century Italian peasant, and carries a flute.*

GEORGE. (*Loudly and with clear articulation*.) Faith, we may put up our pipes and begone.

ARTHUR. What?

GEORGE. Oh, am I wrong? I heard my cue, so I came on.

ARTHUR. Well, kindly go off.

GEORGE. Yes. Still, you gave me my cue, you know. You can't say you didn't.

ARTHUR. What is your cue?

GEORGE. Well, it's really a pause, when everyone's stopped speaking.

ARTHUR. My dear Mr. –

GEORGE. Chudleigh. George Chudleigh.

ARTHUR. My dear Mr. Chudleigh, if every time there's a pause in the play you're going to come on to the stage and speak that line, it's going to make the plot rather difficult to follow –

GEORGE. I meant that's just my cue to come on. My real cue is 'High will' –

JACK. (*Unruffled.*) 'Move them no more by crossing their high will.' He's quite right, Mr. Gosport. (*To* GEORGE.) That *is* your cue, but your line doesn't come till the next act and you ought to have been paying more attention. Now will you please get off the stage as we're rather busy.

GEORGE. Well – that's all very well, but you said it, you know. I heard it quite distinctly. So of course I thought you'd cut a bit out and so I counted five and on I came.

ARTHUR. (*In a fury of impatience.*) Get off the stage, you silly old man –

GEORGE. (*Stolidly indignant.*) Here. Don't you talk to me like that, young chap. I acted with your father.

ARTHUR. I don't care if you acted with Garrick's father. Get off the stage!

GEORGE. You'd better be careful, young feller, talking to people like that. It's not right.

DAME MAUD *now intervenes.* EDNA, *on her balcony, is sitting down, her back to the commotion, reading a newspaper.*

DAME MAUD. You say you acted with my brother?

GEORGE That's right. In this play I was, too. I played Peter.

DAME MAUD. Yes, I remember now. I remember you well. You were just as incompetent then as you are now.

GEORGE. (*Under his breath.*) That's enough from you, you old bag!

DAME MAUD. (*Triumphantly.*) There you are! That shows exactly why you've never got on in the theatre. If you have a line like that to say, you don't mouth it and throw it away, you say it right out. It's a glorious word to say – bag. (*Enunciating.*) Form the word with your lips, like that. BAG. B-A-G. B – A – G.

ARTHUR. All right, Auntie Maud. All right. (*To* GEORGE.) Look, my dear chap, just go to the wings – there's a good fellow – and wait for your scene, which doesn't come for hours yet, while we get on with our work.

GEORGE. I certainly won't. I've been insulted and I'm leaving.

ARTHUR. Nonsense. You can't leave.

GEORGE. Oh yes, I can. I know my rights. What's more, I'm not just leaving, I'm retiring. I'm sixty-seven and I'd have been fifty years on the stage, come April.

DAME MAUD. My dear Mr. – er – you really mustn't take on like this just because –

GEORGE. (*Brushing her aside.*) I've never been a good actor, and when I look at some that are, I thank God for it. What's more I've never liked the life – and I've never needed the money. Why I've gone on all these years mucking about with never more than a line or two to say, sharing dressing rooms with chaps I detest is more than I can fathom. Well, I'm finished with it all now, anyway. Finished with it for good, and you don't know how happy that makes me feel. Goodbye, all.

He goes off. There is a silence after he has gone, broken by DAME MAUD.

DAME MAUD. (*Scornfully.*) Can't even make an exit properly.

EDNA. Must have a film job.

ARTHUR. Oh. All right. One of the supers can do the pipes line. Break for an hour for tea, but don't strike this set. I want to rehearse the farewell scene before the show.

JACK. Yes, Mr. Gosport. (*Calling.*) Break for an hour for tea, everyone! Back at 5.30, please! Curtain up at 7.30.

ARTHUR. Then I'll rehearse the duel.

JACK. Yes, Mr. Gosport.

ARTHUR. And I could see those girls for *The Winter's Tale*.

JACK. Yes, Mr. Gosport.

ARTHUR. And then, if there's time, I can rehearse the jig.

JACK. Yes, Mr. Gosport. (*He goes towards wings.*)

DAME MAUD. Oh, Jack – send someone out for some sandwiches for me – and a bottle of Guinness, would you?

JACK. Yes, Dame Maud.

DAME MAUD. Better make it a couple of bottles. It's so good for my back.

JACK. Yes, Dame Maud.

JACK *goes off.*

DAME MAUD. Goodbye, my children. I'm sure from what I've seen it's all going to be splendid.

Exit.

JOHNNY *comes on with sandwiches for* ARTHUR, *and then goes out.*

ARTHUR. Sandwich, dear?

EDNA. (*To* ARTHUR.) No thank you, darling. I'll have a proper tea for us in our room, my darling.

ARTHUR. Thank you, darling.

EDNA. Don't worry, my precious. That wig is a dream. And you can do your little jump if you want to.

ARTHUR. No, thank you, darling. Edna – I'm not too old for the part, am I?

EDNA. No; of course not, my angel. Or, if you are, then I am.

ARTHUR. But you're three years younger, aren't you?

EDNA. What's three among so many?

She goes out through her bedroom window.

Enter JOHNNY.

Two young men, dressed as HALBERDIERS *and trailing spears, cross the stage at back, chatting to each other in confidential whispers.*

ARTHUR. Johnny, draw the tabs and rehearse some of the lighting cues during the break, will you. (*Over the footlights.*) Miss Fishlock? Would you come to my room for a moment? I want you to take some notes on *The Winter's Tale*. (*He turns and sees the young men.*) Would you come here, you two? (*They both obey with alacrity.*)

(*To one of them.*) Just say – Faith, we may put up our pikes and begone.

FIRST HALBERDIER. (*In a flat, faintly Cockney accent.*) Faith, we may put up our pipes and begone.

ARTHUR. (*To the other.*) Now you.

SECOND HALBERDIER. (*Going much too far, vocally and in gesture.*) Faith, we may put up our pipes and begone.

ARTHUR. (*Pointing to* FIRST HALBERDIER.) Right. You'll do it.

FIRST HALBERDIER. (*Transported.*) You mean – I'm going to have a line to say, Mr. Gosport?

ARTHUR. Yes. (*He hands him the script.*) I'll rehearse you in a few minutes.

MISS FISHLOCK *comes on.*

Ah, Miss Fishlock. Would you get in touch with the London Office at once and inform Mr. Wilmot that the six girls he sent up specially for *The Winter's Tale* are quite out of the question.

MISS FISHLOCK. Yes, Mr. Gosport.

FIRST HALBERDIER. Oh, Mr. Gosport! (*To* SECOND HALBERDIER.) Oh bad luck, Cyril.

Exit MISS FISHLOCK *and* ARTHUR.

SECOND HALBERDIER. (*They drift away, peering at the script together.*) I bet it was because you picked up his gloves at the station on Friday.

He disappears.

FIRST HALBERDIER *looks round the stage cautiously, and finding himself alone, goes down to the footlights.*

FIRST HALBERDIER. (*In a hoarse whisper, across the footlights.*) Mum! Mum!

JACK *appears, unseen by the* HALBERDIER.

I've got a part. It's only a line, but it's awfully important . . . Yes, isn't it wonderful?

JACK. (*Approaching him.*) Who are you talking to?

FIRST HALBERDIER. (*Confused.*) Oh, Mr. Wakefield. I didn't see you. It's only my mother. She's up there. (*He waves towards the upper circle.*)

JACK. Then I'm afraid you must ask her to go. You know the rule about strangers in front at rehearsal.

FIRST HALBERDIER. Oh, but can't she stay and hear me speak my line?

JACK. No, I'm afraid not. She'll have to come back at 7.30 when we start.

FIRST HALBERDIER. But she has to get back to Birmingham tonight. She only came for the day –

JACK. (*Firmly.*) I'm extremely sorry, but rules are rules and Mr. and Mrs. Gosport are very strict about this particular one. She shouldn't be here at all.

He turns away as a man in the costume of Tybalt (FREDERICK INGRAM) *comes on to the stage with a cup of tea and a sausage roll.*

INGRAM. (*To* JACK.) What the hell does he want me for?

JACK. The duel.

INGRAM. Oh, my God! Not again!

The FIRST HALBERDIER *has meanwhile been gesticulating*

*across the footlights to his mother, making uncomplimentary
and furtive gestures towards* JACK. *When he has conveyed his
meaning he goes off.*

I'm slipping across to the Feathers for a quick one. Do you think
I've got time?

JACK. Yes, Mr. Ingram. I'll warn you.

INGRAM *goes off. The assistant stage manager* (JOHNNY)
puts his head on.

JOHNNY. 'Ere – there's a baby in a pram in the wings. Is that a
prop in the play?

JACK. Not unless they've considerably rewritten it. Is it alive?

JOHNNY. Oh, I don't know. I'll just see.

*His head momentarily disappears. We hear, faintly, a baby's
gurgle.* JOHNNY'S *head reappears.*

Yes. It's alive. What shall I do with it?

JACK. I suppose you'd better leave it there. Presumably it belongs
to someone. My God! What with Mums in front and babies in
the wings it's not so much a dress rehearsal as old home week.

*A nondescript, rather shabbily dressed girl of about twenty
(MURIEL), accompanied by a* SOLDIER, *about ten years
older, have come timidly on to the stage and are staring about
them.* JOHNNY'S *head has meanwhile disappeared.*

Yes? What do you want?

MURIEL. (*In a strong Midland accent.*) Could I speak to my Dad,
please?

JACK. And who may your Dad be?

MURIEL. He's an actor.

JACK. Then I'm afraid you've come to the wrong theatre. Try the
Palace of Varieties across the street.

MR. BURTON, *the theatre manager, has come on.*

BURTON. Good evening, Mr. Wakefield.

JACK. Good evening, Mr. Burton.

BURTON. I hope you find our theatre to your satisfaction.

JACK. How are our bookings?

BURTON. Not bad. Not half bad, considering what the show is.
Of course, we've never had these two up here before, you

know, but it's a big help that feller Fred Ingram being in that picture at the Super.

MURIEL. (*To* JACK.) Look – I'm sure it *is* this theatre –

JACK. No, my dear. They've got a sort of circus here this week. The Palace is what you want. Through that door there, up the stairs and into the street.

He moves away again. MURIEL *and the* SOLDIER *go off slowly.*

BURTON. Funny for them to choose to open up here, I must say –

JACK. Social purpose, Mr. Burton.

BURTON. Social purpose? Now what the blazes is that when it's at home?

JACK. As far as I can see it means playing Shakespeare to audiences who'd rather go to the films; while audiences who'd rather go to Shakespeare are driven to the films because they haven't got Shakespeare to go to. It's all got something to do with the new Britain and apparently it's an absolutely splendid idea.

ARTHUR *comes on, now in a dressing-gown.*

Here's Mr. Gosport. He can tell you all about it. This is Mr. Burton, sir. The theatre manager.

ARTHUR. Oh, how do you do? My wife and I are simply thrilled to be opening in your beautiful theatre and this delightful town.

BURTON. Thank you, Mr. Gosport, and I can assure you it's a great honour for us all to have you both up here.

ARTHUR. Thank you. As a matter of fact you've always been very kind to us here in Sheffield –

BURTON. But it's next week you're playing Sheffield, Mr. Gosport.

ARTHUR. Oh! What's this town, then?

BURTON. Brackley.

ARTHUR. Oh yes, of course. They added a week, didn't they? How idiotic of them!

BURTON. That's all right, Mr. Gosport. Great men are always a bit absent-minded.

ARTHUR. Brackley. Of course it is. (*With a sudden change of expression.*) Brackley! Good lord!

JACK. What's the matter?

ARTHUR. I was just remembering something. Brackley! Good heavens!

JACK. Is anything wrong, Mr. Gosport?

ARTHUR *is lost in a reverie.* BURTON *looks at* JACK *a trifle bewildered.* JACK *touches his forehead.* BURTON *nods.*

ARTHUR. Tell me, Mr. – er – hrrhm – , is there a square place in your town with a perfectly repulsive building in glazed brick with a ridiculous dome on top?

BURTON. (*Doubtfully.*) The Civic Centre?

ARTHUR. (*Impatiently.*) Yes, yes. And then, dead opposite, is there an enormous white concrete and glass object that looks just like a public lavatory?

BURTON. (*Too hurt even to protest.*) The Civic Library, Mr. Gosport.

JACK. (*Hastily.*) Do you know this town, then, Mr. Gosport?

ARTHUR. Yes. Only too well.

JACK *manages to get in a nudge.*

Only too well. I was here as a boy in repertory.

BURTON. When exactly were you here, Mr. Gosport? (*Getting out notebook and pencil.*) Could you pin it to a definite date? I ought to ring up the *Argus* about this.

ARTHUR. Well, let me see now. (*He ponders deeply.*) Yes, I can tell you exactly. It was the year Gladys Cooper opened in *The Sign of the Door.*

BURTON. I'm afraid I don't remember that, Mr. Gosport. (*To* JACK.) Do you?

JACK. No. (*To* ARTHUR.) I suppose you couldn't remember anything else that happened that year? A war, or something like that?

ARTHUR. No, I don't think there was a war. Wait a moment – I do remember something that happened that year. There was some sort of commotion –

JACK. A commotion? An earthquake?

ARTHUR. No, no. Something to do with trains. They didn't run. And newspapers too. There weren't any notices. And then I was made to drive a tram, for some reason –

JACK. 1926. The general strike.

ARTHUR. Thank you. That's right. That's what it was called. The general strike.

BURTON. (*Writing down the date*.) 1926.

ARTHUR. Excuse me . . . I must get a cup of tea before I look at six girls . . .

He goes off.

BURTON. Bit scatter-brained, isn't he?

JACK. I doubt if you can scatter a void.

BURTON. I thought he was supposed to be an intellectual sort of chap.

JACK. He's an actor, Mr. Burton.

BURTON. Now perhaps you wouldn't mind giving me a bit more dope on the Gosports for the *Argus*.

JACK. All right, but very quickly. I've got a hundred things to do.

BURTON. How long have they been married?

JACK. Fifteen years.

BURTON. Any children?

JACK. One – little Basil –

BURTON. Oh. And how old is little Basil?

JACK. Thirteen.

BURTON. Up here?

JACK. No. At school –

BURTON. Going to be an actor too?

JACK. Judging by his behaviour, yes. Besides – he's a Gosport.

BURTON. I see. Now how would you describe these Gosports? Would we offend anyone if we called them the most famous married couple in the theatre?

JACK.You wouldn't offend the Gosports, Mr. Burton, which is the main thing. Besides it's reasonably true.

BURTON. Always act together, don't they?

JACK. Yes.

BURTON. Always as husband and wife?

JACK. No. Usually as lover and mistress. The audience prefers that – it gives them such a cosy feeling to know they're really married after all.

BURTON. Now, about this tour. How long is it?

JACK. Sixteen weeks out, then London –

BURTON. Oh. They *are* going to London, then?

JACK. Only for four weeks. If you play in the West End for longer than that you become commercial.

BURTON. I see. What after that?

JACK. Belgrade, Bucharest, Warsaw, Riga, and Moscow.

BURTON. Oh. What about the Iron Curtain?

JACK. The Gosports could make any curtain rise.

BURTON. What plays are they taking?

    ARTHUR, *tea in hand, wanders on and begins fussing mildly in the background, removing a pot of artificial flowers from one place on the stage and putting it in another; then changing his mind and putting it back again.*

JACK. *Romeo, The Winter's Tale, Macbeth,* and a modern play in verse called *'Follow the Leviathan to My Father's Grave'.*

BURTON. What's that about?

JACK. Here's Mr. Gosport, he'll tell you.

BURTON. What's the new play about, Mr. Gosport?

ARTHUR. Death. My wife's got the best part in it. I only play the pencil-sharpener in the last act.

    He replaces the pot once more and wanders off.

BURTON Well, perhaps he'll tell more about it to the *Argus* critic.

JACK. I doubt it.

    ARTHUR *reappears.*

ARTHUR. There's a baby here, in the wings. It looks exactly like someone I know. Who is it?

JACK. I've no idea, I'm afraid.

ARTHUR. It's very careless of people, leaving babies in the wings. There might be a very nasty accident. Somebody might easily trip over it and ruin their exit. See that it's removed before rehearsal.

JACK. Yes, Mr. Gosport.

ARTHUR. And in future, if people bring babies to the theatre, see that they're kept in the proper place.

JACK. Yes, Mr. Gosport. Where's that?

ARTHUR. I don't know.

He goes off again.

JACK. Well, is there any more help I can give you, Mr. Burton?

BURTON. No, thanks. I think that's all. It only remains for me to
wish you a very successful opening, which I'm sure you'll have.

JACK. Thank you very much.

They shake hands. MURIEL *and her* SOLDIER *appear suddenly on Juliet's balcony.*

MURIEL. (*Attacked with vertigo.*) Oo – Tom! Look where we've
got ourselves to!

JACK. Madam – will you and your friend kindly leave this theatre?

MURIEL. No, I won't. I've told you. I want to see my Dad.

JACK. And I've told you your Dad isn't here.

MURIEL. Oh, yes, he is. He's not at The Palace, like you said.
He's here. I've seen his name on the posters.

JACK. Well, you can't see him now, anyway. Anyway. who is your
Dad?

MURIEL. Gosport's the name.

JACK. Gosport?

MURIEL. Yes. Arthur Gosport. He's an actor.

JACK. Oh. I see.

He signs urgently to the prompt corner. JOHNNY *appears.*

So you're the daughter of Arthur Gosport, are you?

MURIEL. Yes, that's right. And this is my husband.

TOM. How do?

JACK. I'm most delighted to meet you both. I simply can't
apologize enough for having been so very rude. (*To* JOHNNY.)
Oh, Johnny. This lady is Mr. Gosport's daughter, and this is her
husband. Would you be so kind as to – er – look after them
both? Just – er – show them around, would you?

*He makes a quick, violent gesture of his thumb, unseen by the
two on the balcony.* JOHNNY *nods.*

JOHNNY. O.K., Mr. Wakefield.

He goes off.

JACK. Now, Miss Gosport –

MURIEL. (*Giggling.*) Mrs. Palmer.

JACK. I do beg your pardon, Mrs. Palmer. Now, if you and your husband would be so very kind as to step through that window there and down the steps, you'll find such a nice gentleman who's going to take such very good care of you both.

MURIEL. Oh. Thanks – you're a pal. Come on, Tom.

She disappears from view. TOM *waves cheerfully to* JACK *and follows her.*

BURTON. Lor' love us! What will they think up next?

JACK. Amazing, isn't it?

BURTON. (*Shaking his head, sadly.*) It's a funny world ours, isn't it?

JACK. Side-splitting.

The FIRST HALBERDIER *comes on mouthing and muttering anxiously to himself.*

BURTON *exits.*

JACK *shakes his head wearily. Then looks at his watch.* JOHNNY *reappears.*

All right?

JOHNNY. I'll lock 'em in one of the downstairs rooms. I'd better not shove 'em out as the doorman's off and they might get in again.

JACK. Quite right. Which room will you put them in?

JOHNNY. I'll put them in number three. There are six other girls there waiting for someone.

JACK. (*Wearily.*) I wonder whose daughters they are. O.K., Johnny. Thanks.

He goes off as the HALBERDIER *approaches* JACK.

HALBERDIER. Mr. Wakefield, do you think it ought to be: Faith, we may put up our PIPES and begone, or FAITH, we may put UP our pipes and begone?

JACK What about, Faith, we may put up our pipes and (*Roaring.*) BEGONE?

HALBERDIER. That doesn't sound quite right to me.

JACK. It sounds awfully right to me. What's happened to your mum?

HALBERDIER. Oh, she's gone.

JACK. (*Grimly.*) That's very lucky for *her*.

> *A very good-looking, smartly dressed girl* (JOYCE LANGLAND) *appears on the stage and stands, evidently a little awed by her surroundings.*

> *The* HALBERDIER *wanders off, still muttering.*

JOYCE. Jack –

JACK. (*Surprised.*) Joyce! (*He approaches her and kisses her warmly.*) Why on earth didn't you let me know you were coming up?

JOYCE. I didn't have time.

JACK. What do you mean, you didn't have time?

JOYCE. I've got some news for you which I had to tell you myself, so I just jumped on the first train.

JACK. Oh, darling! How wonderful!

JOYCE. (*Disappointed.*) You've guessed.

JACK. Your father's changed his mind. Darling, you're a magician. How did you work it?

JOYCE. You worked it. He was terribly impressed with your letter.

JACK. So he should be.

JOYCE. Then I told him your war record.

JACK. That was a mistake, wasn't it?

JOYCE. You got the D.F.C.

JACK. Only because the C.O. liked the pantomime I produced for the chaps. I say, darling, are we rich?

JOYCE. We'll pay super-tax, anyway.

JACK. Oh, darling, how marvellous! I don't have to work any more?

JOYCE. Not in the theatre, anyway.

JACK. Oh. But I do have to work?

JOYCE. He's going to take you into the firm.

JACK. Oh. I thought there was a catch.

JOYCE. Darling, it's not a catch. Jack – it's not that you don't want to give up the theatre, is it?

JACK. Good lord, no! I'd give up the theatre tomorrow if I could.

JOYCE. Well, now you can.

There is a pause, broken by the HALBERDIER *who has wandered on to the stage a few seconds before.*

HALBERDIER. Faith, we may put up OUR pipes and begone.

JACK. Look, old chap – do you mind awfully going and doing that somewhere else? I've got things on my mind.

HALBERDIER. Sorry, Mr. Wakefield. This is my great chance, you know – and I don't want to muck it up. (*Muttering.*) That's it. I know. Faith, we may put up OUR pipes and begone.

He goes off.

JACK. Darling, I think I'd better finish the tour.

JOYCE. (*Horrified.*) The whole tour – forty-six weeks?

JACK. No, no. Only England. After London they'll have to get someone else. But I can't let them down without fair warning.

JOYCE. No. I see that. There's only one thing I'm frightened of though, Jack. Shall I tell you what it is?

JACK. That I haven't the guts to leave them at all?

JOYCE. It's not only the Gosports I'm worrying about. It's the theatre.

JACK. The Gosports are the theatre. There is no theatre apart from the Gosports.

JOYCE. Darling, don't exaggerate.

JACK. I'm not. I mean the Gosports are eternal. They're the theatre at its worst and its best. They're true theatre, because they're entirely self-centred, entirely exhibitionist, and entirely dotty, and because they make no compromise whatever with the outside world.

JOYCE. Then what about this idea of theirs of theatre with a social purpose?

JACK. Theatre with a social purpose, indeed! It's a contradiction in terms. Good citizenship and good theatre don't go together. They never have and they never will. All through the ages, from Burbage downwards, the theatre – the true theatre – has consisted of blind, anti-social, self-sufficient, certifiable Gosports. The point is that if I have the courage to leave the Gosports, I have the courage to leave the theatre.

JOYCE. And have you?

JACK. Yes. I hate the theatre. I shall leave the theatre without the faintest regret, and for a week afterwards I shall barely draw a sober breath in celebration.

JOYCE. (*With a sigh of relief.*) And I'll be at your side in that. Good. Will you go and tell them now, then?

JACK. Now?

JOYCE. Yes. There's a break on, isn't there?

JACK. (*Slowly.*) Yes. Is this a test of my courage?

JOYCE. That's it.

JACK. All right. I might as well get it over with. Besides, I'm giving them plenty of notice, aren't I?

JOYCE. (*Smiling.*) Yes. Plenty.

JACK. (*Annoyed.*) I'm not in the least afraid of them, you know, if that's what you think.

EDNA, *in dressing-gown and chewing a sandwich, wanders on from the wings.*

EDNA. I'm a bit worried about the balcony, Jack. It seems very wobbly to me.

JACK. It's being seen to, Miss Selby. Er – Miss Selby –

EDNA. (*Turning.*) Yes?

JACK. Could I introduce Miss Langland?

EDNA. Oh yes. How do you do? (*She shakes hands.*) You're a serving wench, aren't you?

JACK. Er – no. She's not in the company at all. As a matter of fact, Miss Selby – she's the girl I'm going to marry.

EDNA. Marry! My dear, how wonderful! How simply wonderful! Oh, Jack, darling, I'm so glad. (*She embraces him warmly. To* JOYCE.) And you too, my dear. (*She kisses her.*) So pretty you are, and so young and what an enchanting little frock! Oh, I'm so happy for you both, I feel I want to cry and ruin my make-up. Arthur must be your best man, and I'll be godmother to your first. When's the wedding to be?

JACK. (*Exchanging glances with* JOYCE.) After the provincial tour – when we come to London.

EDNA. Oh, good! (*To* JOYCE.) It would have been far too long a time to wait for him, wouldn't it – forty-six weeks?

JOYCE. (*Surprised.*) Yes. I did feel that, I'm afraid.

EDNA. Don't be afraid, dear. You're quite right to be impatient. I was, when I married Arthur. (*She strokes* JOYCE'S *face.*) Dear little child. I'm so happy for you. So you'll be coming to Europe with us, will you?

JOYCE. Er – no, Miss Selby. I won't.

EDNA. No? Well, perhaps you're wise. It's going to be rather uncomfortable for all of us, I expect. Still, won't you miss him, being gone all that time?

JACK. Well – the fact is, Miss Selby – you see – I – er – well – this is the point – I'm not sure that I'm going to Europe myself.

EDNA. Not going to Europe? (*She looks mildly surprised then appears to see daylight.*) Oh, I know what you mean. Some nasty creature must have sneaked to you about what Arthur was saying the other day about Ronnie Williams coming to stage-manage for us. But you mustn't worry, my darling. It was only because Ronnie Williams stage-managed for us for so long – practically before you were born, my darling – and Arthur heard he was out of a job, and you know how tactless he is, the poor old thing – but he really didn't mean it, I know he didn't –

JACK. (*Desperately.*) Look, Miss Selby – it's got nothing to do with Ronnie Williams –

EDNA. You're hurt, my precious. I'm so sorry. But I can promise you most faithfully that there was never, never any question of our not taking you to Europe. We all love you and admire you far too much –

JACK. Thank you very much, Miss Selby, but –

EDNA. Now I don't want to hear anything more about it. Just forget the whole thing and pretend it never happened. You're coming with us to Europe. I promise you. Goodbye, you dear things. (*She blows them a fond kiss.*) You look so pretty, the two of you, standing there together.

She goes off.

JACK. (*To* JOYCE.) Look, darling, perhaps a dress rehearsal isn't the best moment to break it to them. What about tomorrow – or after the first night?

JOYCE. Or after Sheffield, or after London, or after the European tour? No, Jack, darling, something tells me that if you don't do it now, during this break, you never will –

JACK. I could write them a letter –

JOYCE. I thought you said you weren't afraid of them?

ARTHUR *wanders on and makes straight for the flower pot, removing it, in the background, to another spot.*

JACK. I know. I'll tell *him*. He's really much easier to deal with than she is.

JOYCE. (*Indicating* ARTHUR.) Well, now's your chance, then.

JACK *starts violently; then braces himself and takes* JOYCE *by the hand up to* ARTHUR.

JACK. Oh, Mr. Gosport.

ARTHUR. Yes.

JACK. Could I introduce Miss Langland?

ARTHUR. Oh. How do you do. Have you read *The Winter's Tale?*

JOYCE. Er – no. I'm afraid I haven't.

ARTHUR. Well, it's not a difficult part. It's about a girl who's abandoned by her father when she's a baby, and then many years later they meet –

JACK. Er – Miss Langland isn't here about *The Winter's Tale,* Mr. Gosport. (*In a firm, measured voice.*) She's my fiancée, we're getting married after the provincial tour, and I'm not coming with you to Europe.

ARTHUR. Yes. I see, my dear fellow. Now what about those girls for *Winter's Tale?* Are they here?

JACK. Yes, I think so. Did you hear what I said, Mr. Gosport?

ARTHUR. Yes, of course. I think I'd better see those girls straight away. Have them in, one by one, would you? (*He puts the pot in another place.*)

JACK. Yes, Mr. Gosport. (*Calling.*) Johnny. Are the girls here for *Winter's Tale?*

JOHNNY.(*Off.*) Yes. Seven of them.

JACK. That's right. Mr. Gosport will see them now, separately.

JOHNNY.(*Off.*) O.K.

ARTHUR. (*Indicating pot.*) How do you like it here, Jack?

JACK. Much better.

ARTHUR. (*To* JOYCE.) What do you think, Miss – er – Hrrhm?

JOYCE. I think it's charming, there.

ARTHUR. No. I don't think I like it there very much. (*He removes it.*)

JACK. Mr. Gosport, I don't think you quite grasped what I said just now.

ARTHUR. (*Annoyed at the implication.*) Of course I did, my dear fellow. You said you thought the pot looked better there, but I don't agree –

JACK. No. Before that. I told you I was getting married –

ARTHUR. Getting married? I'm absolutely delighted, my dear chap. (*He shakes hands.*) Who to?

EDNA *comes on.*

ARTHUR. Edna, I've thought of an entirely new way of dying.

EDNA. Have you darling? How exciting.

ARTHUR. Bring on the tomb, someone.

JACK. Yes, Mr. Gosport. (*Calling.*) Johnny, give me a hand with the tomb.

JOHNNY. (*Coming on.*) Yes, Mr. Wakefield.

He and JACK bring forward the tomb and JOHNNY goes off.

ARTHUR. (*Going over to* JOYCE.) Now, young lady perhaps you would be kind enough to take up a position there – thank you. (*To* EDNA.) The beauty of it is in its simplicity. Now I must get you something to lie on.

He takes a mackintosh from JOYCE *and spreads it over the tomb.* EDNA *lies on it.*

Thank you.

JACK. Look, Mr. Gosport, there's something I've got to tell you before you die.

ARTHUR. Well, if she can't do the quick change in time, she'll just have to wear the black velvet all through.

JACK. But Mr. Gos –

ARTHUR That's all there is to it. I don't want to hear another word about it. (*Adopting his dying pose.*)

Now. Come, bitter conduct, come, unsavoury guide!
Thou desperate pilot, now at once run on,
The dashing rocks thy sea-sick weary bark!
Here's to my love! (*Drinks.*) – Oh true apothecary!
Thy drugs are quick. – Thus with a kiss I die.

And a very spectacular death it is. JOYCE, *despite her prejudice, is thrilled.*

JOYCE. (*To* JACK.) That was wonderful!

ARTHUR. (*Overhearing.*) Oh, did you like it, Miss – Hrrhm? I'm
so glad. You didn't think it was too much?

JOYCE. Oh no. Not a bit – I thought it was thrilling.

EDNA. (*Sitting up.*) Jack, darling, don't you think your little friend
must be feeling awfully cold, standing on this draughty stage in
that thin little frock? Wouldn't she be much better off in a nice
warm dressing-room?

JACK. (*Resignedly.*) Yes, Miss Selby. (*To* JOYCE.) Darling, run
along to my room, would you? It's number fourteen on the
second floor. I'll join you when I can.

JOYCE. All right. (As *she goes.*) Now, don't let me down, Jack.
Before the break is up.

EDNA. Such a sweet little face.

JACK. Before the break is up. I promise.

JOYCE *goes out.*

EDNA. Arthur, it's a lovely death, but I'm not absolutely sure it
doesn't go on perhaps a hair too long. I don't think we'll put it
in tonight.

ARTHUR. (*Knowing he has lost.*) All right, darling. I just thought
it was worth trying – that was all.

The HALBERDIER *comes on, still muttering.*

HALBERDIER. Oh, Mr. Gosport. Are you ready for me yet?

ARTHUR. No. In a minute. I'm seeing some girls first. Just wait
there.

He motions him to a corner of the stage, where the HALBERDIER
sits, mouthing intermittently.

All right, Jack. Ready for *The Winter's Tale.*

JACK. (*Calling.*) All right, Johnny. Send the first lady on, will
you?

JOHNNY. (*Off.*) O.K.

JACK. (*Calling.*) What is the lady's name, please?

Whispers off.

JOHNNY. (*Off.*) Muriel Palmer.

JACK. (*Writing it down.*) Muriel Palmer.

And MURIEL PALMER *comes on, followed at a few yards' interval by her* SOLDIER HUSBAND. JACK, *busy with his notebook, does not immediately look up.*

MURIEL. (*With a joyous cry, pointing at* ARTHUR.) There he is! That's my Dad! Daddy, I'm your daughter, and you're my Dad.

ARTHUR. Er – what text are you using, Miss, er – hrrhm?

JACK. (*Interposing quickly.*) Excuse me, Mr. Gosport, but I know about this young lady. She's been annoying us all the evening. (*To* MURIEL.) How did you get out of that room?

MURIEL. A young man came and unlocked us and told me and six other girls to come on the stage separately as Mr. Gosport was waiting for us –

JACK. Oh God! All right. Well, now, are you going to go quietly or shall I have to ring up for the police?

MURIEL. Ring up the police? Go ahead. I don't mind. I haven't done anything wrong. I just want a few words with my Dad, that's all. That's my Dad, all right. I recognize him from Mum's picture on the piano.

TOM. Even in this country you can't arrest a girl for talking to her Dad, you know.

MURIEL. You can't scare me, young man.

JACK. All right. (*Calling.*) Johnny! Ring up the police station and ask them to send a man round. We're having trouble.

ARTHUR. (*To* JACK.) Do I understand that this lady claims that I'm her father?

MURIEL. Your name is Gosport, isn't it?

ARTHUR. Arthur Gosport. Yes.

MURIEL (*Chattily.*) Well, I'm your daughter, Muriel. You've never seen me, because I was born after you left Mum. This is my husband, Tom – he's your son-in-law.

TOM. How do?

MURIEL. And I've brought someone else along that I thought you'd like to meet. Tom! (*She signs to him to go to the wings.*)

TOM. O.K., Mu.

ARTHUR. Just a minute. (*To* MURIEL.) You mentioned just now a character called Mum. Could you be more explicit, please? Where does this Mum person live?

MURIEL. Same old place. Number twenty-one Upper Brecon Road.

ARTHUR. Opposite a puce, rectangular building – with a notice board outside, saying Thy Days are Numbered?

MURIEL. That's right. The Baptist Chapel.

ARTHUR. And is Mum's name – Florence?

MURIEL. Flossie. That's right.

ARTHUR. (*Whimpering.*) Flossie! (*With a wail.*) Oh, no, no. It can't be!

MURIEL. Oh yes, it is, Dad.

EDNA. Arthur! You can't mean –

ARTHUR. Yes, yes, oh yes! It's true. I know it now. (*Pointing tragically.*) You've only to look at her face to see it. The living image of her dreadful mother.

MURIEL. Well, really! That's a nice way to talk, I must say –

JACK. (*Taking charge.*) Look, Mr. Gosport – as we've never seen the lady's dreadful mother, perhaps there's some other way we could test her story. (*To* MURIEL.) When were you born?

MURIEL. January 15th, 1927.

JACK. (*To* ARTHUR.) When did you last see Flossie?

ARTHUR. Don't cross-examine me! I don't know. I can only tell you that I am absolutely convinced of the truth of this girl's statement. This is my daughter, Mabel –

MURIEL. Muriel. Mu for short.

ARTHUR. My daughter, Muriel. Mu for short.

He sinks down on to a stool, his head in his hands. EDNA *loyally goes to his side to comfort him.*

(*To* MURIEL.) Why are you here? What do you want?

MURIEL. Want? I don't want anything. Just to say hullo, that's all. It seemed silly being in the same town, and for us not even to meet each other. Mum didn't want me to come, but I thought Dad'll be interested to see what I look like, and to meet his son-in-law. Besides I've got such a nice little surprise for you. (*Calling.*) Come on, Tom. I want to introduce you to your grandson.

TOM *appears, wheeling a pram tenderly towards the group, who are too frozen with horror to move.*

ARTHUR. (*At length* .) My – grandson?

MURIEL. That's right, Dad. Come and look.

Very slowly ARTHUR *rises and, with* EDNA *on one side and* JACK *on the other, gazes down on the pram.* MURIEL *and* TOM *complete the group. There is a long pause.*

ARTHUR. (*Slowly, at length.*) It looks – (*With a sob.*) – like Beerbohm Tree –

EDNA. (*Hopelessly.*) No, darling. The terrible thing is – it looks awfully like you.

ARTHUR. Don't say that, Edna!

MURIEL. Yes, he's the image of his Grandpa, isn't he? The ickle, chicka-widdy-biddy woo. Go on, Grandpa, tickle his little tummy.

ARTHUR. I refuse to tickle his little tummy.

EDNA. (*To* TOM.) How old is it?

TOM. Five months. You're Edna Selby, aren't you?

EDNA. Yes.

TOM. I saw you in Shakespeare once, in Birmingham. You were the Queen, weren't you, when Mr. Gosport was Hamlet?

EDNA. I have played it – yes.

TOM. (*Cheerfully.*) Well then in a sort of way, that makes you our little Ted's great-grand-mama, doesn't it?

EDNA. No, it doesn't. Not in any sort of way, and please, don't say it does. (*Reproachfully.*) Arthur – how could you!

ARTHUR. (*Pointing to the pram.*) I am not responsible for Ted.

EDNA. (*Pointing to* MURIEL.) But you are responsible for Mu.

ARTHUR. (*Tragically.*) I was a mere boy – a wild, hotheaded, irresponsible, passionate boy – a Romeo of seventeen –

EDNA And your Juliet was Flossie.

ARTHUR. She was my landlady's daughter. I loved her, for a time, with all my heart and mind. She loved me too, in her way – but not enough. She never even came to the theatre to see me act. Of course it had to end, as all such mad, youthful follies must.

EDNA. (*Pointing to the pram.*) It didn't have to end in this.

ARTHUR. And I say unto you, the sins of the fathers shall be visited upon the children even unto the third and fourth generation. You know the line –

EDNA. It seems to have got up to the fourth generation far too quick. (*Pointing to the pram*.) Oh, Arthur, it's not in my nature to reproach you for what is past and done, but I do think you've been terribly, terribly foolhardy. (*To* TOM.) Please remove this.

TOM. O.K. If that's the way you feel –

MURIEL. (*To* BABY.) Didn't they appreciate him, then? Come along, then, my ickywicky-chick-a-boo! (*She begins to wheel the pram out*.) Come along, then! Say ta-ta for now, Grand-daddy –

ARTHUR. (*Sinking again into an attitude of tragic despair*.) Oh, my God! Edna! What am I to do?

Once more EDNA *takes his hand in silent but loyal sympathy*.

The PALMERS *wheel their baby out*.

There is a pause, broken by the HALBERDIER, *who, throughout the preceding scene, has been mouthing intermittently in the background, more or less oblivious of what has been going on*.

HALBERDIER. (*Attempting a new reading*.) Faith, we may put UP our PIPES and begone.

ARTHUR. Jack, what am I to do?

JACK. (*Reassuringly*.) Well, Mr. Gosport, they haven't bothered you at all for twenty years. I don't see any reason why they should in the future.

ARTHUR. Yes – but that child! (*With a shudder*.) That horrifying child!

JACK. No one need know about that. Ask your dau – Mrs. Palmer, to keep the whole thing secret; and if I might venture to suggest it, send an occasional little present to them for the baby.

EDNA. A nice little box of jujubes, flavoured with prussic acid.

ARTHUR. I don't think it's in quite the best of taste to make a joke of that sort, Edna. After all, the creature is my grandson. (*In agony again*.) Oh, God! my grandson!

EDNA. Never mind, my darling. These things can happen to any of us.

ARTHUR. But why, when I'm playing Romeo of all parts? Why couldn't it have turned up when I was playing Lear?

EDNA. That's life, my darling.

ARTHUR. Of course we shall have to cancel the performance now.

JACK. Look, Mr. Gosport – I really don't think you'll find it necessary to do that –

ARTHUR. How can I play a boy of seventeen with a grandson in the wings, mocking me with that repulsive leer of his, every time I go on?

JACK. Because it won't be in the wings. First thing tomorrow morning I shall go and see – er – Mrs. Palmer's mother. I'd better have her address again.

ARTHUR. Twenty-one Upper Brecon Road

JACK. (*Writing it down.*) Thank you. And what is her name?

EDNA. Flossie.

JACK. I know. I meant her surname.

ARTHUR. Gosport, I suppose.

JACK. Gosport?

EDNA. What an odd coincidence!

JACK. Mr. Gosport – did you – did you marry Flossie?

ARTHUR. Oh yes. She made rather a point of it, I remember.

EDNA. Arthur! You mean your daughter isn't illegitimate?

ARTHUR. Oh no. She's perfectly legitimate, I think.

EDNA. (*Annoyed.*) Well, really? Of course that puts an entirely different complexion on the whole thing. It's going to make *me* look very silly – if that gets out.

ARTHUR. It all happened such a long time ago, darling, and I really didn't see why I should bother you with the whole, rather sordid, story.

JACK. (*Quietly.*) Mr. Gosport – when did you divorce your first wife?

ARTHUR Let me see, now. I left her to take a part in a revival of *The Passing of the Third Floor Back* at Barnes.

JACK. I said, when did you divorce her? This is rather important. You did divorce her, didn't you?

ARTHUR. Yes, of course I did, my dear fellow. I remember perfectly.

JACK. Did you divorce her or did she divorce you?

ARTHUR. We divorced each other, my dear chap.

JACK. In law that isn't quite possible, Mr. Gosport. Who was awarded the decree nisi – you or your wife?

ARTHUR. Decree nisi? What's that?

JACK. It's the decision awarded by the judge in a divorce action.

ARTHUR. A judge? I don't remember a judge. I'm sure if there'd been a judge, I'd have remembered. There was a solicitor – I know that – and a lot of documents to sign –

JACK. (*His voice becoming gradually edged with horror as the truth becomes clearer.*) Mr. Gosport – one solicitor and a lot of documents don't make a divorce, you know.

ARTHUR. My dear fellow, don't fuss! Everything was perfectly legal and in order, I assure you.

JACK. You don't think it might just have been a deed of separation that you signed, and not a divorce at all?

ARTHUR. Of course it was a divorce. It must have been a divorce. The solicitor's name was Jenkins. He had Commissioner of Oaths on his glass door, I remember.

MURIEL *and her* SOLDIER *wander on.*

MURIEL. Hullo, Dad. Just been having a look round the stage. Don't mind, do you?

JACK. (*Urgently.*) Mrs. Palmer, if I ask you a straight question, will you please give me a straight answer?

MURIEL. All right. Fire away.

JACK. Is your mother divorced?

MURIEL. Divorced? Mum? Of course not.

JACK. (*Quietly.*) Thank you. That was what I had already gathered.

MURIEL. Mind you, she's often thought of divorcing Dad, but somehow never got round to doing it. Not that she's got a good word to say for him, mind you. She says he was the laziest, pottiest, most selfish chap she's ever come across in all her life. 'He'll come to a sticky end,' she used to say to me, when I was a little girl. 'You mark my words, Mu,' she used to say, 'if your Dad doesn't end his days in gaol my name's not Flossie Gosport.'

JACK. Your mother, Mrs. Palmer, is plainly a remarkable prophetess. Would you and your husband mind returning to No. 21 Upper Brecon Road as I have a rather important little matter to discuss with your Dad, who will be getting in touch with you in due course.

MURIEL. O.K. Well, ta-ta for now, Dad.

ARTHUR. Ta-ta and I will arrange for three complimentary seats to be left in your name for the Thursday matinée.

TOM. Thanks a million, Dad.

ARTHUR. I'm not your Dad, you know.

TOM. In law, old cock, in law.

MURIEL *and* TOM *go off.*

There is a pause, after they have gone.

EDNA. (*To* ARTHUR.) Darling, I must say it looks as if you've been very, very careless.

ARTHUR. Darling, there must be some hideous mistake. The whole thing is absolutely ridiculous. Jack, you must fix it.

JACK. Mr. Gosport and Miss Selby – I'm afraid this is something that not even I can fix. You must face, both of you, a very unpleasant fact. You are bigamously married.

There is another pause.

ARTHUR. (*Calling.*) Miss Fishlock!

MISS FISHLOCK. (*Off.*) Yes, Mr. Gosport.

ARTHUR. Come here a moment, would you?

MISS FISHLOCK *comes in, notebook and pencil at the ready.*

Miss Fishlock, it appears that my wife and I have committed bigamy. You'd better ring up the London Office at once and inform Mr. Wilmot.

MISS FISHLOCK. (*Faintly.*) Yes, Mr. Gosport. What – did you say – you and your wife have committed?

ARTHUR. Bigamy.

MISS FISHLOCK *sways slightly and is supported by* JACK. *Then clutching her pencil firmly, she bravely writes down the fatal word – or its shorthand equivalent.*

MISS FISHLOCK. Yes, Mr. Gosport.

EDNA. Silly word, isn't it? It sounds almost as if Arthur and I had committed a serious crime –

JACK. I hate to alarm you, Miss Selby, but that that is exactly what Mr. Gosport has committed.

ARTHUR. You mean, I might have to pay a fine – or something like that?

JACK. (*Gently.*) Miss Fishlock, do you happen to know the maximum penalty for bigamy?

MISS FISHLOCK *nods, biting her quivering lower lip.*

ARTHUR. What is it, Miss Fishlock?

MISS FISHLOCK. (*In a whisper.*) Imprisonment – for life.

There is a stunned silence.

EDNA. And – does that apply to me too, Miss Fishlock?

MISS FISHLOCK. No, Miss Selby. You haven't committed any crime – (*Nearly in tears.*) – only Mr. Gosport.

EDNA. (*Aghast.*) They wouldn't *separate* us?

JACK. I'm afraid they would, Miss Selby.

EDNA. Oh, no, they wouldn't. They couldn't. If Arthur has to go to prison, I shall go too.

JACK. I doubt if that is allowed, Miss Selby. Is it, Miss Fishlock?

MISS FISHLOCK. No, Mr. Wakefield. I don't know of any – prison – where – convicts – are allowed to take their wives with them –

The thought is too much for her. She bursts frankly into tears and runs into the wings.

ARTHUR. (*Calling after her.*) Miss Fishlock! Miss Fishlock! What an idiotic woman, to get so hysterical!

EDNA. (*Approaching him and hugging him.*) Oh, my darling, I won't let them take you from me. I won't! I won't!

ARTHUR. Darling, there's nothing at all to get so worked up about. I'll make a public apology, divorce Flossie properly, and marry you again.

EDNA. But that would be such horrible publicity –

ARTHUR. The Arts Council will fix that. (*Suddenly galvanized into life.*) Now don't let's waste any more time. We've got to get to work.

His eye lights on the HALBERDIER *who, all this time, has been patiently sitting in the background waiting to be called for rehearsal.*

You! I'll do your line now. (*To* EDNA.) Darling, do you mind taking up your position in the potion scene, after you've drunk the potion.

While ARTHUR *is placing* EDNA *where he wants her for the scene,* JACK *goes up to the* HALBERDIER.

JACK. My God! How much did you hear of all that?

HALBERDIER. Oh, that's all right, Mr. Wakefield, I'm not a tattle-tale. Wish me luck, Mr. Wakefield. This is my great chance –

ARTHUR. (*Turning.*) All right, Mr. – Hrrhm. We're ready for you. Now, I'll give you your cue.

HALBERDIER. Thanks, Mr. Gosport.

ARTHUR. Leave a five-second pause, come on, look down at the bed and see what you take to be a dead body. Now I want to get from your expression that you realize that this girl, at whose wedding you have been hired to play, has taken her own life, presumably because she couldn't face her marriage with Paris, and that she has died for love of another. Your face should express understanding of the undying conflict between spiritual love and this gross, mundane world.

HALBERDIER. Gracious!

ARTHUR. Well, if you can't do it, just look sad. Then turn and say your line to your fellow musicians who we presume to be off-stage, there. (*He points.*) Understand?

HALBERDIER. Yes, Mr. Gosport.

ARTHUR. All right. Go off, Jack, music.

The HALBERDIER *runs off.*

JACK. Panatrope.

ARTHUR. The heavens do lower upon us for some ill.
Move them no more by crossing their high will.

After the correct time interval, the HALBERDIER *comes on, acting hard. He gazes down at* EDNA, *and contrives to look very sad, sighing deeply and shaking his head. Then he turns slowly and faces* GEORGE CHUDLEIGH, *who has come on silently behind him.*

HALBERDIER.
GEORGE.   } Faith we may put up our pipes and begone.

ARTHUR What? Oh Mr. Hrrhm – you've come back.

GEORGE. I just felt I couldn't desert you both in the hour of your great affliction.

ARTHUR Our great affliction?

JACK. Oh, my God! How did *you* hear?

GEORGE. I was in The Feathers, and a chap in the company came in and told us all how Mr. and Mrs. Gosport were likely to get a life-sentence for bigamy –

JACK. Oh, God! The news must be half over Brackley by now –

He runs off.

EDNA. (*Calling after him.*) Don't worry, Jack. The company, I know, will stand by us. (*To* GEORGE.) Mr. Chudleigh, it was naughty of you to leave us so suddenly, but I think I know what was the matter – we all of us suffer from an occasional *crise de nerfs*.

CHUDLEIGH. *Crise de* what!

EDNA. Nerves, Mr. Chudleigh, nerves. Now come with me and I'll give you a nice strong cup of tea.

They go off together.

ARTHUR, *during this, has been staring, chin in hand, fixedly at the set. The* HALBERDIER *has been staring fixedly, and despairingly, at him.*

HALBERDIER. Mr. Gosport?

ARTHUR. Yes?

HALBERDIER. Do you want me any more?

ARTHUR. What? Oh, no, thank you.

FIRST HALBERDIER. You couldn't – let me have another line to say – some time – could you?

ARTHUR. (*Abstractedly.*) I'll keep you in mind.

HALBERDIER. (*Sadly.*) Thanks, Mr. Gosport.

ARTHUR *goes off.* JACK *comes back.*

JACK. Too late! It's out of The Feathers and into the Green Horse, now. They've all heard it.

JACK *wearily subsides on the stool. The* HALBERDIER *approaches him timidly.*

HALBERDIER. Mr. Wakefield?

JACK. Yes?

HALBERDIER. Do you think I should give up the theatre?

JACK. Why ask me?

HALBERDIER. You know so much about Life.

JACK. What has Life got to do with the theatre?

HALBERDIER. (*He wanders to the wings.*) It's an awful shame about that line. It came at such an important time, with Miss

Selby and Dame Maud on, and after a pause and with a chance
for face-acting. The London critics might have noticed me –

JACK. (*Sympathetically.*) I rather doubt that. The potion scene
comes very soon after the interval.

HALBERDIER. Well, cheeribye.

JACK. Cheeribye.

The HALBERDIER *goes out sadly.*

JOHNNY S VOICE (*Off.*) Mr. Wakefield!

JACK. (*Calling.*) Yes, Johnny?

JOHNNY'S VOICE. (*Off.*) The lady in your dressing-room says
I'm to tell you time is getting on and you're not to forget your
promise.

JACK. (*Calling.*) All right. Thank you.

Enter DAME MAUD.

DAME MAUD . What is this terrible news?

JACK. Oh, Dame Maud, have you been to The Feathers!

DAME MAUD. I just looked in for a little refreshment and heard
this abominable slander. Jack, have some pity on an old lady
and tell me it isn't true.

JACK. I'm afraid it is true, Dame Maud.

DAME MAUD. I see. Well of course I suppose you know who's at
the bottom of it all, don't you?

JACK. No. Who?

DAME MAUD. The Old Vic.

JACK. Oh, I don't think so, Dame Maud.

DAME MAUD. Why dear Jack, are you quite blind? It's as clear as
daylight to me. They stick at nothing, that lot, absolutely
nothing. I'm going to ring them up this moment and tell them
exactly what I think of them.

JACK. No, Dame Maud, you mustn't. You. really mustn't.

DAME MAUD. And Sadler's Wells.

DAME MAUD *goes off followed by* JACK.

The stage is empty a moment, and then a uniformed POLICE-
MAN *walks on from the wings with firm measured tread. He
looks round him.* JOHNNY, *still busy on the balcony, comes on.*

POLICEMAN. Who's in charge here, please?

JOHNNY. Mr. Wakefield. He'll be back in a minute.

After shaking the balcony once more JOHNNY *goes off.* JACK *comes on and stops dead at sight of the* POLICEMAN.

JACK. (*Murmuring.*) Oh God!

POLICEMAN. You Mr. Wakefield?

JACK. That's right, yes. Yes, I'm Mr. Wakefield, officer. Yes, that's quite correct.

POLICEMAN. I understand you want assistance.

JACK. Assistance?

POLICEMAN. One of your chaps rang up to say you were having bother at the theatre.

JACK. (*Infinitely relieved.*) Oh, that! Oh yes. Of course, I'd forgotten. (*He laughs, rather hysterically.*) Well, well, well! Just fancy your taking all that trouble to come round here. I do think that's good of you, officer – but as a matter of fact it was all a mistake – an utter misunderstanding –

POLICEMAN. You're not having any bother?

JACK. Oh, no, no, no! No bother in the world. Not a trace of bother. Everything's quite, quite perfect.

POLICEMAN. Then I don't know what you're doing wasting our time –

JACK. Oh, my dear old chap – I can't tell you how sorry I am about that. It's awful to think of you walking all that way from the police station on a wild-goose chase. Look, sit down, my dear fellow, do. (*He brings up a stool.*) Make yourself comfortable and I'll get you a nice drink. A nice large drink. What would you like? Whisky?

The POLICEMAN *nods.*

Yes. I thought you would. Now just stay there. Don't move, will you? There are all sorts of dangerous contraptions in a theatre and you might hurt yourself and that'd be dreadful. Just sit there and relax and I'll dash and get you an enormous zonk of whisky –

He goes off, still burbling.

The POLICEMAN, *sitting patiently on the stool, is evidently rather surprised at the extreme affability of his reception. There is a pause, then* DAME MAUD *crosses the stage, another glass of Guinness clutched in her hand. She does not at first see the* POLICEMAN. *When she does she utters one single hoarse and strangled scream, and sinks slowly to the floor in a dead faint. The* POLICEMAN *rises, startled, as* JACK *comes back with a whisky.*

POLICEMAN. Here, quick! There's an old lady having a fit –

JACK. What? Oh, it's Dame Maud. Oh lord! I suppose she saw you – I mean – she goes off at the slightest thing, you know. (*Calling.*) Johnny,Johnny! Come here, quick!

JOHNNY *comes on.*

Give me a hand with Dame Maud.

JOHNNY. Took queer, is she?

JACK. Just one of her dizzy spells –

POLICEMAN. I'd better lend a hand – I know my first aid.

JACK. Oh no. Please don't bother. You really mustn't trouble yourself, officer. It's nothing at all. She's always doing this. She's over a hundred, you know   poor old thing. Just sit down and be comfortable, and pay no attention at all.

DAME MAUD. (*As she is carried off.*) Get me a drink, for God's sake!

JACK *and* JOHNNY *carry her into the wings.*

The POLICEMAN *settles down once more on his stool. There is another pause and* EDNA *comes on quickly.*

EDNA. Jack – are we doing the farewell –

She sees the POLICEMAN *and stands quite motionless looking at him as he rises politely. Then, very slowly, she walks towards him.*

(*Sadly, resignedly, and melodiously.*) Ah, well. There is no purpose to be served, I suppose, in kicking against the pricks.

POLICEMAN. Beg pardon, ma'am?

EDNA. Constable – I only want to say one thing. In fifteen years my husband and I have never spent a single night apart –

POLICEMAN (*Politely.*) Is that so, ma'am? Just fancy!

EDNA. Not one. If we were separated, I think we would die.

POLICEMAN. Would you indeed, ma'am?

EDNA. I want you to know that nothing can keep us apart. Nothing; and no one – not even you, constable – can come between us now. If you take him, you must take me too.

POLICEMAN. (*After a pause, stunned with bewilderment.*) I see, ma'am. I'll bear that in mind.

JACK comes back and gasps as he sees EDNA *with the* POLICEMAN.

JACK. Oh, Miss Selby, Dame Maud has been taken a bit faint. She's calling for you urgently.

EDNA. (*Tragically.*) What can that matter now? I've been telling the constable –

JACK. (*Hastily.*) Isn't it nice of the constable to come dashing round just because he heard we were having a little trouble in the theatre – especially when we're not having any trouble at all – are we?

EDNA. (*Understanding slowly.*) Oh. Oh, I see. Constable, dear constable, perhaps you'd better forget what I said just now –

POLICEMAN. I'll try to, ma'am, I'm sure.

EDNA. Just a little secret between the two of us, eh? (*To* JACK.) What a beautiful line of the neck the constable has, hasn't he, Jack?

JACK. Beautiful.

POLICEMAN. Here, I say!

EDNA. Goodbye, constable, and thank you for your great, great kindness to us all. I shall never forget it.

She goes off.

POLICEMAN. That was Edna Selby, wasn't it?

JACK. Yes, officer. You mustn't, you know, pay too much attention to anything she might have said to you. She's suffering from the most terrible first-night nerves.

POLICEMAN. Oh, is that the way it takes them?

JACK. Nearly always. Now, if you've quite finished your drink, I'd better escort you out –

POLICEMAN. Thanks. I can find my own way out –

JACK. Oh. Well, it's rather complicated and I wouldn't like you to be bothered by any of the other actors.

POLICEMAN. Are they all suffering from first-night nerves, then?

JACK. Nearly all of them. Come along, officer. I'll just clear a way for you –

He and the POLICEMAN *move to the wings.* JACK *goes out.*

The POLICEMAN *goes back for his helmet, which, in his confusion, he has left by the stool.* ARTHUR *comes in.*

ARTHUR. (*Explosively.*) Well, really, inspector. This is too much! I do think you might have waited until after the performance.

POLICEMAN. Well – Mr. Gosport, sir, I've got my work to do – you see –

ARTHUR. But, my dear inspector, you mustn't listen to a word my wife says. I can assure you we're divorced. There's no doubt at all about it.

POLICEMAN. Is that so, sir? I'd no idea.

ARTHUR. And anyway, we haven't spoken a single word to each other since the general strike.

POLICEMAN. That's too bad, sir. Your wife gave me to understand quite different –

ARTHUR. Of course she would, my dear fellow. She's out for publicity, I suppose. But I'll tell you something else, my dear chap. (*Confidentially.*) I'm not at all sure that my child is really mine –

POLICEMAN. Good gracious!

JACK *comes back in a hurry.* ARTHUR *goes up to balcony.*

JACK. My God! Mr. Gosport, Miss Selby's ready for the farewell. Officer, come this way, please! Please come this way! (*He drags the* POLICEMAN *away from* ARTHUR. *In a low voice.*) You mustn't pay any attention to him either. Least of all to him.

POLICEMAN. First-night nerves too?

JACK. Far worse than that. He's completely and utterly off his rocker. It's terribly, terribly sad –

POLICEMAN. Lor' love us! But he can still act?

JACK. Yes, he can still act. That's all he can do. Come along, officer, please.

He gets him off the stage.

JOHNNY *has come on to the balcony and is attaching a rope ladder to it.* ARTHUR *and* EDNA *appear on the balcony.*

JOHNNY *goes off, shaking his head.*

ARTHUR Give me the lighting for the farewell, please.

The light comes down to give a rosy dawn effect.

All right. Let me be ta'en, let me be put to death;
I am content, so thou wilt have it so.
I'll say yon grey is not the morning's eye,
'Tis but the pale reflex of Cynthia's brow;
Nor that is not the lark, whose notes do beat
The vaulty heaven so high above our heads:
I have more care to stay than will to go:
Come, death, and welcome! Juliet wills it so.
How is 't, my soul? Let's talk; it is not day.

EDNA. It is, it is; hie hence, be gone, away!
It is the lark that sings so out of tune
Straining harsh discords and unpleasing sharps.
Some say the lark makes sweet division;
This doth not so, for she divideth us;
Some say the lark and loathed toad change eyes;
O! Now I would they had chang'd voices too,
Since arm from arm that voice doth us affray,
Hunting thee hence with hunts-up to the day.
O! now be gone; more light and light it grows.

ARTHUR. More light and light; more dark and dark our woes.

MISS FISHLOCK *suddenly flies on from the wings, and her
countenance, transported with joy, is suffused with the rosy
gleams of the sun now rising on Verona.*

MISS FISHLOCK. (*In great excitement.*) Mr. Gosport – Miss
Selby – I know you'll forgive me for interrupting you. I have
important news.

ARTHUR. Yes, Miss Fishlock?

MISS FISHLOCK. I got through to Mr. Wilmot and gave him your
message. He was most calm, most kind, most helpful, and most
reassuring. He is coming down to Brackley tomorrow morning
by an early train in person.

EDNA. How very good of him!

MISS FISHLOCK. What is more he gave me a message to pass on
to you both. He says you are on no account to worry yourselves
about this matter. He says he happens to know there can be no
danger whatever of – of – what we feared –

ARTHUR. (*Triumphantly.*) I knew it!

MISS FISHLOCK. He says it will probably be necessary for Miss
Selby to sign a document saying that at the time she married
you, Mr. Gosport, she was aware that you were already married.
That, of course, would have the effect of making your second
marriage null and void.

ARTHUR. Oh. That's splendid!

MISS FISHLOCK. There can therefore be no question of your having committed an offence in law. Oh, Mr. Gosport, he was so wonderfully brave. He went on to say that there should be little difficulty in your getting a divorce from this – this other person. Then, afterwards, should you and Miss Selby still wish it, you could get married again. Only no publicity, of course. And that, of course, would settle the entire problem once and for all. (*She beams gladly at the balcony, conscious of a duty well performed.*)

EDNA. How brilliant he is, isn't he, Arthur? I really don't know why anybody ever works for another management.

ARTHUR Thank you, Miss Fishlock. You've done extremely well. I'm very grateful.

MISS FISHLOCK. I knew you'd both be pleased. Oh, Mr. Gosport – I'm so glad – I really am. I do congratulate you. And you too, Miss Selby.

EDNA and ARTHUR. (*Murmuring.*) Thank you, Miss Fishlock.

MISS FISHLOCK *goes off, again in tears, but this time, of joy.*

EDNA. Arthur, don't you think you ought to say a few words to the Company? I know they'll all be overjoyed at the news.

ARTHUR Oh. Very well. (*Calling.*) Jack, assemble the Company, would you?

JACK *appears.*

JACK. They're mostly in front already, Mr. Gosport. (*Looking at front of house.*) Remain in your seats down there – everyone else on, please.

ARTHUR. Oh, right. (*To the House.*) Ladies and Gentlemen. With regard to this subject of bigamy – the danger point is past. I am sure you will be delighted to hear that Mr. Wilmot has discovered a way by which my marriage to Miss Selby can be rendered entirely illegal –

There is a little flutter of handclapping from the wings.

Thank you very much. Nor would it be right to let this occasion pass without extending on your behalf, on Miss Selby's and on mine, our most grateful thanks to Mr. Wilmot, without whose co-operation and – ingenuity – and savoir-faire – this very happy result would barely have been possible.

Another outburst of applause, louder than the first. Mr. Wilmot's spies, one feels, are everywhere.

Also to Miss Fishlock, who, as usual, has had to do most of the donkey-work, and has done it, as always, far better than anyone would ever expect.

One solitary clap for MISS FISHLOCK.

And lastly, Ladies and Gentlemen, to yourselves for the great loyalty you have shown in this moment of crisis to my wife, that is to say, Miss Selby, and myself. A thousand thanks. And one other thing. I'm not a difficult man in the theatre, as you know, but I would like to have it perfectly clear that I consider a very great deal of time has been wasted during this break for tea. Please see that it doesn't occur again. And now – back to work.

ARTHUR *goes off.*

EDNA. Just a moment, everyone. I also have an announcement to make. I know you will all be overjoyed to hear that Miss Fishlock with characteristic ingenuity has at last successfully completed the National Insurance forms for the entire company.

Enter ARTHUR.

ARTHUR. Bravo. (*To* EDNA.) Let's just finish the climb down, my dear.

EDNA. Yes.

ARTHUR *climbs on to ladder.*

Since arm from arm that voice doth us affray,
Hunting thee hence with hunts-up to the day.
O! now be gone; more light and light it grows.

ARTHUR. More light and light; more dark and dark our woes.

EDNA. Then, window, let day in, and let life out.

ARTHUR. Farewell, farewell! one kiss, and I'll descend.

He begins to climb down.

EDNA. Art thou gone so? Oh Arthur – I've just thought of something quite, quite dreadful.

ARTHUR. What?

EDNA. Little Basil.

ARTHUR. Little Basil? (*Calling.*) Miss Fishlock!

MISS FISHLOCK *flies on again.*

MISS FISHLOCK. Yes, Mr. Gosport?

ARTHUR. Ring up Mr. Wilmot immediately and inform him that he appears to have made little Basil into a little bastard –

MISS FISHLOCK. Yes, Mr. Gosport.

She goes off.

ARTHUR. What's more there's far too much light on this scene –
don't you agree, dear?

EDNA. Yes, dear, I do. Especially on the balcony.

ARTHUR. (*Calling.*) Jack!

JACK comes on.

There's too much from here and too much from there. (*Waving
his arms to left and right.*) Now is everyone ready?

JACK. You can't get the lights much lower than this, Mr. Gosport,
or they'll go out altogether –

ARTHUR. Nonsense, my dear fellow.

*The tabs draw revealing the Verona scene with the TWO HAL-
BERDIERS GEORGE CHUDLEIGH, and INGRAM grouped.*

Now – are we all here? I just want to do the duel.

DAME MAUD comes on to the balcony.

DAME MAUD. As you've stopped, dear, I thought you wouldn't
mind if I gave you another teeny little hint –

EDNA Not just now, Auntie Maud. Do you mind? Perhaps
tomorrow –

DAME MAUD. Tomorrow will be far too late.

EDNA (*Paying no attention.*) There's still too much on the balcony,
Jack.

JACK. (*Shouting.*) Bring it down more, Will! It'll never stand it,
Miss Selby.

EDNA. I'm sure it will – the lights never let us down.

ARTHUR (*In Verona.*) Now, Tybalt, take the villain back again
That late thou gav'st me; for Mercutio's soul
Is but a little way above our heads,
Staying for thine to keep him company;
Either thou, or I, or both, must go with him.

INGRAM. Thou wretched boy, that didst consort him here,
Shalt with him hence.

ARTHUR. This shall determine that.

INGRAM. What! Art thou drawn among these heartless hinds?
Turn thee – look upon thy death!

JOYCE. (*Shouting above the din.*) Jack! Jack! Time's up.

JACK. What? Oh, clear the stage, will you, darling? We're extremely busy.

JOYCE. No. I won't. Have you told them yet?

JACK. Told them what? Oh that. No, I haven't. Look, darling, I'm afraid you'll have to wait for me, that's all. I can't leave these two now. I realize that. How can I let them go behind the iron curtain without one sane man to look after them?

JOYCE. Sane? You're not sane! You're as mad as they are. This madhouse has infected you too.

JACK. Madhouse? This isn't a madhouse. It's just an ordinary dress rehearsal, that's all – now clear the stage, darling.

EDNA. Jack, dear, there's still too much light on this balcony.

JACK. If you take the lights down more than this, Miss Selby, they'll fuse.

EDNA. Let them fuse.

ARTHUR. (*Still in Verona.*) Again, please. That's too quick.

JOYCE. It's no good, Jack, I'm leaving you. You'll never get out of this, it's bedlam, and you're in it for life. Goodbye, Jack, goodbye.

She runs off the stage.

JACK. Joyce!

DAME MAUD. (*Looking down from the balcony.*) Now that girl has talent. Who is she? Arthur – who was that girl?

ARTHUR. (*Still arranging the fight in Verona.*) I don't know, Auntie Maud. Get her name, will you, Jack?

JACK. I've got her name, Mr. Gosport. It's Joyce Langland. She was my fiancée.

ARTHUR. Good. We'll try her for *Winter's Tale* tomorrow. Now this duel is getting very sloppy. Let's go back.

EDNA. There's still too much light, Jack.

JACK. Yes, Miss Selby. Take it down more, Will. And try those thunder and lightning cues 2, 3, and 4.

The lights suddenly go out.

My God! They've fused.

Summer lightning is now playing fitfully on the scene.

ARTHUR. (*Calling*.) House lights. House lights.

The house lights go up. MR. BURTON *rushes on.*

BURTON. (*In a frantic voice*.) Take those lights out! It's seven thirty. There's an audience in front. Look!

He points. A row of startled faces gaze at the now visible audience, and then they scatter in panic to the wings.

The house lights go out. There is a moment's black-out, disturbed by summer lightning and a roll of thunder. Then the stage lights come on again, revealing an empty stage. ARTHUR *comes on slowly carrying his pot.*

JACK. (*Off, whispering frantically*.) Mr. Gosport! Mr. Gosport! The audience is in front.

He beckons him to the wings. Other faces and other beckoning figures appear, but ARTHUR *is oblivious. He walks slowly round the pot, then, dissatisfied with its appearance, picks it up once more and walks slowly out, to the strains of the overture.*

The curtain falls.